Reality *is* *a* Hypothesis

Jayesh Bapu Ahire

22nd June, 2018

Preface

Dedicated to my family, friends and all those people who supported me at every moment of my life.

Table of Contents

Introduction

SCIENCE has revealed much about the world and our position within it. Generally, the findings have been humbling. The Earth is not the centre of the universe. Our species descended from brutes. We are made of the same stuff as mud. We are moved by neurophysiological signals and subject to a variety of biological, psychological and sociological influences over which we have limited control and little understanding.

One of our remaining sources of pride is technological progress. Like the polyps that over time create coral reefs, the many generations of humans that have come before us have built up a vast technological infrastructure. Our habitat is now largely one of human making. The fact of technological progress is also in a sense humbling. It suggests that the most advanced technology we have today is extremely limited and primitive compared with what our descendants will have.

If we extrapolate these expected technological advances, and think through some of their logical implications, we arrive at another humbling conclusion: the "simulation argument", which has caused some stir since I published it three years ago.

The formal version of the argument requires some probability theory, but the underlying idea can be grasped without mathematics. It starts with the assumption that future civilisations will have enough computing power and programming skills to be able to create what I call "ancestor simulations". These would be detailed simulations of the simulators' predecessors – detailed enough for the simulated minds to be conscious and have the same kinds of experiences we have. Think of an ancestor simulation as a very realistic virtual reality environment, but one where the brains inhabiting the world are themselves part of the simulation.

The simulation argument makes no assumption about how long it will take to develop this capacity. Some futurologists think it will happen within the next 50 years. But even if it takes 10 million years, it makes no difference to the argument.

Let me state what the conclusion of the argument is. The conclusion is that at least one of the following three propositions must be true:

1. Almost all civilisations at our level of development become extinct before becoming technologically mature.

2. The fraction of technologically mature civilisations that are interested in creating ancestor simulations is almost zero.

3. You are almost certainly living in a computer simulation.

How do we reach this conclusion? Suppose first that the first proposition is false. Then a significant fraction of civilisations at our level of development eventually become technologically mature. Suppose, too, that the second proposition is false. Then a significant fraction of these civilisations run ancestor simulations. Therefore, if both one and two are false, there will be simulated minds like ours.

If we work out the numbers, we find that there would be vastly many more simulated minds than non-simulated minds. We assume that technologically mature civilisations would have access to enormous amounts of computing power.

So enormous, in fact, that by devoting even a tiny fraction to ancestor simulations, they would be able to implement billions of simulations, each containing as many people as have ever existed. In other words, almost all minds like yours would be simulated. Therefore, by a very weak principle of indifference, you would have to assume that you are probably one of these simulated minds rather than one of the ones that are not simulated.

Hence, if you think that propositions one and two are both false, you should accept the third. It is not coherent to reject all three.

It should be emphasised that the simulation argument does not show that you are living in a simulation. The conclusion is simply that at least one of the three propositions is true. It does not tell us which one.

In reality, we don't have much specific information to tell us which of the three propositions might be true. In this situation, it might be reasonable to distribute our credence roughly evenly between them.

Let us consider the options in a little more detail. Proposition one is straightforward. For example, maybe there is some technology that every advanced civilisation eventually develops and which then destroys them. Let us hope this is not the case. Proposition two requires that there is a strong convergence among all advanced civilisations, such that almost none of them are interested in running ancestor simulations. One can imagine various reasons that may lead civilisations to make this choice. Yet for proposition two to be true, virtually all civilisations would have to refrain. If this were true, it would be an interesting constraint on the future evolution of intelligent life.

The third possibility is philosophically the most intriguing. If it is correct, you are almost certainly living in a computer simulation that was created by some advanced civilisation. What Copernicus and Darwin and latter-day scientists have been discovering are the laws and workings of the simulated reality. These laws might or might not be identical to those operating at the more fundamental level of reality where the computer that is running our simulation exists (which, of course, may itself be a simulation). In a way, our place in the world would be even humbler than we thought.

What kind of implications would this have? How should it change the way you live your life?

Your first reaction might think that if three is true, then all bets are off and you would go crazy. To reason thus would be an error. Even if we are in a simulation, the best methods of predicting what will happen next are still the familiar ones – extrapolation of past trends, scientific modelling and common sense. To a first approximation, if you thought you were in a simulation, you should get on with your life in much the same way as if you were convinced that you were leading a non-simulated life at the "bottom" level of reality.

If we are in a simulation, could ever know for certain? If the simulators don't want us to find out, we probably never will. But if they choose to reveal themselves, they could certainly do so. Another event that would let us conclude with a high degree of confidence that we are in a simulation is if we ever reach a point when we are about to switch on our own ancestor simulations. That would be very strong evidence against the first two propositions, leaving us only with the third.

The Simulation Hypothesis revised

In a paper published in 2003, Nick Bostrom argued that at least one of several propositions is likely to be true:

(1) the human species is very likely to go extinct before reaching a "posthuman" stage, i.e., (f p = 0);

(2) any posthuman civilization is extremely unlikely to run a significant number of simulations of their evolutionary history (or variations thereof), i.e., (f I = 0);

(3) we are almost certainly living in a computer simulation, i.e., (f sim =1)

(4) Proposition is characterized as the simulation hypothesis, thus only a part of Bostrom's simulation

argument. The argument is thus basically a statement of possibilities:

Either ($f_p =0$) or ($f_I =0$) or ($f_{sim} =1$)—such that, Bostrom claims, we should distribute our credence more or less evenly among them. 1 But this leaves us with the problem of justification, i.e., why we should distribute our belief in one or another of these propositions more or less evenly.

Bostrom uses the words "living in" to stipulate that, whatever "we" are is to be understood in terms of the following points concerning a posthuman simulation of present-day humans (Bostrom 2003):

(1) "a computer running a suitable program would be conscious."

(2) "it would suffice for the generation of subjective experiences that the computational processes of a human brain are structurally replicated in suitably fine-grained detail, such as on the level of individual synapses."

(3) "Simulating the entire universe down to the quantum level is obviously infeasible, unless radically new physics is discovered. But in order to get a realistic simulation of human experience, much less is needed – only whatever is required to ensure that the simulated humans,

interacting in normal human ways with their simulated environment, don't notice any irregularities."

(4) "a posthuman simulator would have enough computing power to keep track of the detailed belief-states in all human brains at all times. Therefore, when it saw that a human was about to make an observation of the microscopic world, it could fill in sufficient detail in the simulation in the appropriate domain on an as-needed basis. Should any error occur, the director could easily edit the states of any brains that have become aware of an anomaly before it spoils the simulation. Alternatively, the director could skip back a few seconds and rerun the simulation in a way that avoids the problem."

Despite these observations, Bostrom is not adequately clear how we are to understand the term 'simulation'. For example, we conceive of humans as having "organic" intelligence (assuming here some mind-brain interaction) and distinguish this from "artificial" intelligence. The former is associated with a biological (carbon-based) entity, while Bostom anticipates the latter is of a different material substrate. Bostrom allows for posthumans implementing a process of mechanized intelligence that operates on some kind of material substrate that need not be organic. There would then be a causal relation of orders of being: A simulation, S, (3rd order), i.e., what is being processed, is operationally dependent on a model, M, (2 nd order), i.e., the programming, that represents a reality, R, (1 st order), i.e., what is fundamentally real and, as such, is the presupposition of any model, thus: (R → M → S, i.e., if and only if there is that which is fundamentally real can there then be a model which is the representation of that reality by way of a programming experienced as a simulation). Hence, when he says humans may be "living in" a simulation, Bostrom means that literally: They have their being only as 3rd order artificial intelligence processes and they are not "really" biologically independent organic intelligent entities such as we presently understand the members of the set, Homo sapiens, to be. All that we are, all that we think and do, whether seemingly mental or corporeal activity, all are the manifestations of a simulation, or said otherwise, what posthumans would call "ancestor-simulations."

Bostrom's extended argument presupposes a historical relation between a species of posthumans and contemporary humans, such that

(1) posthumans are objectively real beings (1st order),

(2) contemporary humans are simulated beings (3rd order), while

(3) there is a universe (i.e., a physical reality) that is objectively real (1st order), although the perceived universe of the simulated beings may be nothing more than a simulation. Bostrom conjectures:

> *...later generations...with their super-powerful computers [might] run detailed simulations of their forebears or of people like their forebears...They could run a great many such simulations. Suppose that these simulated people are conscious...[It] could be the case that the vast majority of minds like ours do not belong to the original race but rather to people simulated by the advanced descendants of an original race. It is then possible to argue that, if this were the case, we would be rational to think that we are likely among the simulated minds rather than among the original biological ones.*

He concludes, "Therefore, if we don't think that we are currently living in a computer simulation, we are not entitled to believe that we will have descendants who will run lots of such simulations of their forebears." But there are questions begging here: Why should anyone think we are currently living in a computer simulation? Why would anyone believe, or want to believe, that we will have descendants who will run many simulations of forebears such as ourselves? And how is it that the former proposition entitles one to believe the latter?

Bostrom's simulation hypothesis is one among a number of papers produced in the latter part of the 20th century that concern the same basic question and issues. Jürgen Schmidhuber, for example, reported a few years ago that, "In the 1940s, Konrad Zuse already speculated that our universe is computable by a deterministic computer program (Horst Zuse, personal communication, 2006), like the virtual worlds of today's video games." (Schmidhuber 2012; Zuse 1967) Schmidhuber himself argued that, "Zuse's hypothesis is compatible with all known observations of quantum physics." Linking this hypothesis to its mathematical implications, Schmidhuber added: "Somewhat surprisingly, there must then exist a very short and in a sense optimally fast algorithm that not only computes the entire history of our own universe, but also those of all other logically possible universes." (Schmidhuber 2012)]

Similarly, F. J. Tipler, in his "omega point theory" of 1988-89, conceived of a time in which "there will be sufficient computer capacity to simulate our present-day world by...creating a simulation of all logically possible variants of our world." (Tipler 1997; Tipler 1995) Indeed,

Tipler argued, a simulated person "would observe herself to be as real, and as having a body as solid as the body we currently observe ourselves to have. There would be nothing 'ghostly' about the simulated body, and nothing insubstantial about the simulated world in which the simulated body found itself." Writing in 2004, Gordon McCabe considered Tipler's position as "a special case of epistemological scepticism," Tipler's argument being that, "our experience is indistinguishable from the experience of someone embedded in a perfect computer simulation of our own universe," the logical consequence of which is that, "hence, we cannot know whether or not we are part of such a computer program ourselves." (McCabe 2004)

By contrast, writing in 1989, mathematical physicist Roger Penrose challenged the "strong AI [artificial intelligence]" view of his day that human consciousness can be run on a computer, accounting in his argument for implications of mathematical theorems such as Gödel's incompleteness theorem and empirical understanding in neurophysiology. (Penrose 1989) Given his firm commitment to strong AI research, Tipler recorded his disagreement with Penrose. (Tipler 1989) In short, Bostrom's hypothesis is by no means unusual for many involved with the strong AI school of cognitive studies that herald evolutionary advances in computational methods, to the degree that such simulations are reasonably supported by theoretical considerations.

It is not Bostrom's conclusion that interests us here. Since we do not normally think—and do not find it normatively rational to think—that we are currently "living in" a computer simulation, rather than each human today being an objective, material (biological, organic) reality, then it is by no means problematic to us to be concerned with the likelihood of ancestor-simulations or our logical "entitlement" to any such belief. As a matter of what at the least appears to us to be objectively probable real fact, we may or may not have descendants (posthumans) who will run simulations of humans. There is no epistemological obligation to believe this proposition, although we may entertain it, at minimum, as a prediction having probability value (where truth value=1 and probability-value is >0 but <1).

However, what is of interest to us is Bostrom's proposition (3)—'we are almost certainly living in a computer simulation.' This is not a predictive statement. It is structured (at least initially) as an empirical proposition having high probability value (near 'truth=1')— if Bostrom's reasoning stands the test of critical engagement. Despite the "almost certain" feature of this proposition (f_{sim} =1), Bostrom has stated he believes the probability that this hypothesis is true is less than 0.5; and he adds, "A degree of belief of something like 20% would seem quite reasonable given our current information." (Bostrom 2005b) Notwithstanding, this proposition is sufficiently provocative to elicit our critical engagement, and to engage it critically as a proposition that, if true, presents a necessary and sufficient condition for thereafter considering the normativity of the belief Bostrom proposes in his conclusion.

Here one can concur with several propositions already articulated by Danila Medvedev in 2003 as "necessary assumptions" for Bostrom's simulation argument:

(1) there is a basic reality;

(2) it is possible to run a world simulation inside a reality;

(3) the complexity of the simulation is less than the complexity of the parent universe;

(4) the laws of logic and mathematics are absolute. [Medvedev, no date)

We may also accept as reasonable "several less general assumptions" that Medvedev identifies:

(1a.) the base reality contains at least one [post-]human civilization;

(2a.) a human civilization has non-zero probability of becoming a posthuman civilization; and

(3a.) a posthuman civilization has non-zero chances to launch at least one simulation.

Of course, one may consider whether we have in Bostrom's discourse the presentation of a genuine problem of science, thus whether we may consider his hypotheses scientific, i.e., hypotheses that are "open in some way or other to empirical falsification," thus to empirical testing. Methodologically construed, a hypothesis is "proposed in an attempt to solve some genuine problem or at least to answer some genuine query." (Miller 2007) Consider, for example, Eric Winsberg understanding of 'simulation', when he says that, "Many complex systems in the physical sciences are studied by developing models of their underlying physics on a computer, and by using computationally intensive methods to learn about the behaviour of those systems." (Winsberg 2003) A posthuman running an ancestor-simulation would be doing the same—using computationally intensive methods to learn about the behaviour of "the complex systems" that the species H. sapiens is (or was) in its environmental setting. However, what matters here, as Winsberg clarifies, is that, "the mathematical models that drive these particular kinds of simulations are motivated by theory. Prima facie, they are nothing but applications of scientific theories to systems under the theories' domain." (Winsberg 2003)

Thus, in running an ancestor-simulation, a posthuman would apply scientific theories to those systems that fall under the domain of a given theory. This would include the basics and complexities of contemporary theoretical computer science. Thus, e.g., in considering Zuse's hypothesis (noted above) and considering constraints, Schmidhuber has argued for "a very short algorithm [denominated FAST] that computes all possible universes, as long as they are computable." (Schmidhuber 2012, italics added) He then proposed, "For any God- like Great Programmer, FAST offers a natural, optimally efficient way of computing all logically possible worlds." Indeed, "It our universe is one of the computable ones, then FAST will eventually produce a detailed representation of its first few billion years of local time (note that nearly 14 billion years have passed since the big bang)." (Schmidhuber 2012)

Schmidhuber's conditional proposition is not to be underestimated—this is the basic question: Is our universe (the one we presume to know by way of our sciences) one of the computable ones? Accounting for "the weak anthropic principle," Schmidhuber argues, "Since we exist, we already know that at least one of the programs has computed enough to enable our existence..." He asserts further, "With high probability it will be one of the shortest and fastest compatible with our existence...[We] are already part of one of the simplest, fastest, non-random worlds compatible with our very being." (Schmidhuber 2012) But there is a problem here. This latter statement is true only if it is true that, indeed, our "existence" is a computation-effect—which is precisely the question that goes begging here. It makes no sense to say, "we exist," without qualifying that statement so as to avoid equivocation, thus to mean that the "we" here and the "existence" that is referent here are only expressions for a simulation as such. We also have to explain how or why it is that we would not have, as an effect of computation, a detailed representation of the complete 14 billion years of local time since the Big Bang.

We are pressed, therefore, to consider all the more seriously Richard Feynman's musings about simulating physics with computers, including the physics investigated by quantum theory. (Feynman 1982) Feynman asked, "What kind of computer are we going to use to simulate physics?" Bearing in mind what was known at the time (1982) about digital computing (theoretical computer science), Feynman asked, "Can physics be simulated by a universal computer?" Assuming a posthuman would obviously have a technological sophistication well beyond what was known in 1982 and what is known today (2015), the fact is that, given what we perceive to be physical reality, we would have to say, at minimum, that this is what a posthuman has decided to represent in simulation. This simulation could include whatever physical reality is to be known by way of classical mechanics, relativity, and quantum mechanics (given the current state of theoretical representations of our physical reality).

Feynman argued that, because "the physical world is quantum mechanical...therefore the proper problem is the simulation of quantum physics..." (Feynman 1982) Presumably, a posthuman would face and then solve the same problem theoretically. (Bear in mind that Bostrom has already asserted that, "simulating the entire universe down to the quantum level is obviously infeasible.") Feynman considers "the possibility that there is to be an exact simulation, that the computer will do exactly the same as nature. If this is to be proved...then it's going to be necessary that everything that happens in a finite volume of space and time would have to be exactly analyzable with a finite number of logical operations." There is a problem with this proposal, however, Feynman argued: "The present theory of physics is not that way, apparently. It allows space to go down into infinitesimal distances, wavelengths to get infinitely great, terms to be summed in infinite order, and so forth; and therefore, if this proposition is right, physical law is wrong." This raises questions concerning what a posthuman would be doing in running ancestor-simulations that include

(1) simulated humans

(2) interacting with an environment that

(3) includes "everything that happens in a finite volume of space and time."

Feynman is not averse to the possibility that physical law is wrong (although the probability of this is low to moderate, given present theoretical constructs). Hence, allowing for this possibility of low probability, he considers altering our idea of space: We could have "the idea that space is a simple lattice and everything is discrete (so that we can put into it a finite number of digits) and that time jumps discontinuously." Given these ideas, Feynman proposed a "rule of simulation," viz., "the number of computer elements required to simulate a large physical system is only to be proportional to the space-time volume of the physical system." (Feynman 1982) The question, then, is: What follows from observing this rule, and what might follow with more or less moderate to high probability if we drop the rule for any simulation conceived?

The fact is that we currently have quantum theory as part of the theoretical and experimental apparatus of our survey of physical reality. If posthumans are in fact simulating what we take to be our present reality, then (we would have to say) quantum theory (as we understand or do not understand it) is being simulated. Yet, without explanation, Bostrom already stated that simulating the entire universe down to the quantum level is obviously infeasible. Why is this "obviously" infeasible? Infeasible for whom? For us? Yes, perhaps we should say it is infeasible for us. But, would this be infeasible for a technologically sophisticated posthuman? It seems we can reasonably answer "maybe not," given Bostrom's proposal with his probability value of p~0.2. Of course, Feynman himself argued that, with quantum mechanics "we know immediately that here we get only the ability, apparently, to predict probabilities;" in which case, since "quantum mechanics seem to involve probability," we can ask whether probabilistic theory can be simulated. (Feynman 1982)

Given Feynman's analysis, we would have to say that a posthuman could not simulate by calculating the probability of quantum effects: "We can't expect to compute the probability of configurations for a probabilistic theory," Feynman argued, unless such computation occurs by way of a "probabilistic computer" that simulates a "probabilistic nature" in which "the output is not a unique function of the input." (Feynman 1982) And here, it seems, a posthuman would face a dilemma in computation. Feynman states the problem thus: "You see, nature's unpredictable; how do you expect to predict it with a computer? You can't—it's unpredictable if it's probabilistic." However, a posthuman surely would have the capacity to do what Feynman says one can do:

> But what you really do in a probabilistic system is repeat the experiment in nature a large number of times. If you repeat the same experiment in a computer a large number of times (and that doesn't take any more time than it does to do the same thing in nature of course), it will give the frequency of a given final state proportional to the number of times, with approximately the same rate (plus or minus the square root of n and all that) as it happens in nature. In other words, we could imagine and be perfectly happy, I think, with a probabilistic simulator of a probabilistic nature, in which the machine doesn't exactly do

what nature does, but if you repeated a particular type of experiment a sufficient number of times to determine nature's probability, then you did the corresponding experiment on the computer, you'd get the corresponding probability with the corresponding accuracy (with the same kind of accuracy of statistics).

If we assume a posthuman does what Feynman describes, then there is a way to produce some features of the quantum reality that we currently describe by way of quantum mechanics, in which case the simulation would include both macro-level and quantum-level elements according to the causal relationship (R➜M➜S). This computing ability, however, would not include Fermi particles, says, Feynman, in which case the fact that we do include such particles as elements of current quantum theoretical description means that this counts (for contemporary humans, at least, if not for posthumans) as an empirical fact in the present context of scientific knowledge against the validity of the simulation hypothesis, i.e., it counts as an element in the falsification of the simulation hypothesis.

However, one would have to consider here what computational capacity we expect from a posthuman conducting an ancestor-simulation when the posthuman is spatiotemporally future to the humans being simulated. In his review of Alan Turing's position on machine intelligence in relation to the mathematical objection associated with Gödel's incompleteness theorem, Gualtiero Piccinini cites Turing's observation that, of course, machines have a storage capacity that limits the machine's "adaptability." This then counts against the

ascription of intelligence. (Piccinini 2003) Put in its "aggressive" form, the argument is this: "It has...been shown that with certain logical systems there can be no machine which will distinguish provable formulae of the system from unprovable, i.e., that there is no test that the machine can apply which will divide propositions with certainty into these two classes. Thus if a machine is made for this purpose it must in some cases fail to give an answer."

Turing accordingly argues the point that, "if a machine is expected to be infallible, it cannot also be intelligent. There are several mathematical theorems which say almost exactly that. But these theorems say nothing about how much intelligence may be displayed if a machine makes no pretence at infallibility." Thus, to be fair to his proposal, we must bear in mind that Bostrom allows for a material substrate that enables massive storage. Operating on an assumption in the philosophy of mind, Bostrom says, "The idea is that mental states can supervene on any of a broad class of physical substrates. Provided a system implements the right sort of computational structures and processes, it can be associated with conscious experiences." Bostrom thus accounts for what we currently conceive as "theoretical limits on information processing in a given lump of matter."

Bostrom considers both the computing power and the memory requirements. Concerning the latter, he says: "...since the maximum sensory bandwidth is ~10^8 bits per second, simulating all sensory events incurs a negligible cost compared to simulating the cortical activity. We can therefore use the processing power required to simulate the central nervous system as an estimate of the total computational cost of simulating a human mind." Moreover, Bostrom allows for a technological sophistication such that, "a rough approximation of the computational power of a planetary-mass computer is 10^{42} operations per second, and that assumes only already known nanotechnological designs...A single such a [sic] computer could simulate the entire mental history of mankind (call this an ancestor- simulation) by using less than one millionth of its processing power for one second." Thus, any concern for falsifiability of the simulation hypothesis must account for the probability of a nano-level technological architecture and correlative processing of human mental events.

Despite the foregoing survey of conceptually plausible ideas, we are nonetheless faced with criticisms such as follow from Heidegger's phenomenological analysis of Dasein and what it implies for the difference between computation and thinking. And here, importantly, Bostrom seems to identify the two, based on his reductionist account from the philosophy of mind. Hubert Dreyfus provides a ready contribution that relates to Bostrom's proposal.

Matrix and Philosophy

After a lot of technical in previous article this article will emphasize on analogies between Matrix movie and the theory we are proposing.

A. Dream Skepticism

Neo has woken up from a hell of a dream — the dream that was his life. How was he to know? The cliché is that if you are dreaming and you pinch yourself, you will wake up. Unfortunately, things aren't quite that simple. It is the nature of most dreams that we take them for reality — while dreaming we are unaware that we are in fact in a dreamworld. Of course, we eventually wake up, and when we do we realize that our experience was all in our mind. Neo's predicament makes one wonder, though: how can any of us be sure that we have ever *genuinely* woken up? Perhaps, like Neo prior to his downing the red pill, our dreams thus far have in fact been dreams *within* a dream.

The idea that what we take to be the real world could all be just a dream is familiar to many students of philosophy, poetry, and literature. Most of us, at one time or another, have been struck with the thought that we might mistake a dream for reality, or reality for a dream. Arguably the most famous exponent of this worry in the Western philosophical tradition is the seventeenth-century French philosopher Rene Descartes. In an attempt to provide a firm foundation for knowledge, he began his *Meditations* by clearing the philosophical ground through doubting all that could be doubted. This was done, in part, in order to determine if anything that could count as certain knowledge could survive such rigorous and systematic skepticism. Descartes takes the first step towards this goal by raising (through his fictional narrator) the possibility that we might be dreaming:

"How often, asleep at night, am I convinced of just such familiar events — that I am here in my dressing gown, sitting by the fire —when in fact I am lying undressed in bed! Yet at the moment my eyes are certainly wide awake when I look at this piece of paper; I shake my head and it is not asleep; as I stretch out and feel my hand I do so deliberately, and I know what I am doing. All this would not happen with such distinctness to someone asleep. Indeed! As if I did not remember other occasions when I have been tricked by exactly similar thoughts while asleep! As I think about this more carefully, I see plainly that there are never any sure signs by means of which being awake can be distinguished from being asleep. The result is that I begin to feel dazed, and this very feeling only reinforces the notion that I may be asleep."

When we dream we are often blissfully ignorant that we are dreaming. Given this, and the fact that dreams often seem as vivid and "realistic" as real life, how can you rule out the possibility that you might be dreaming even now, as you sit at your computer and read this? This is the kind of perplexing thought Descartes forces us to confront. It seems we have no justification for the belief that we are not dreaming. If so, then it seems we similarly have no justification in thinking that the world we experience is the real world. Indeed, it becomes questionable whether we are justified in thinking that *any* of our beliefs are true.

The narrator of Descartes' *Meditations* worries about this, but he ultimately maintains that the possibility that one might be dreaming cannot by itself cast doubt on all we think we know; he points out that even if all our sensory experience is but a dream, we can still conclude that we have *some* knowledge of the nature of reality. Just as a painter cannot create *ex nihilo* but must rely on pigments with which to create her image, certain elements of our thought must exist prior to our imaginings. Among the items of knowledge that Descartes thought survived dream skepticism are truths arrived at through the use of reason, such as the truths of mathematics: "For whether I am awake or asleep, two and three added together are five, and a square has no more than four sides."

While such an insight offers little comfort to someone wondering whether the people and objects she confronts are genuine, it served Descartes' larger philosophical project: he sought, among other things, to provide a foundation for knowledge in which truths arrived at through reason are given priority over knowledge gained from the senses. (This bias shouldn't surprise those who remember that Descartes was a brilliant mathematician in addition to being a philosopher.) Descartes was not himself a skeptic — he employs this skeptical argument so as to help remind the reader that the truths of mathematics (and other truths of reason) are on firmer ground than the data provided to us by our senses.

Despite the fact that Descartes' ultimate goal was to demonstrate how genuine knowledge is possible, he proceeds in *The Meditations* to utilize a much more radical skeptical argument, one that casts doubt on even his beloved mathematical truths. In the next section we will see that, many years before the Wachowskis dreamed up *The Matrix,* Descartes had imagined an equally terrifying possibility.

B. Brain in the Vat Skepticism

Before breaking out of the Matrix, Neo's life was not what he thought it was. It was a lie. Morpheus described it as a "dreamworld," but unlike a dream, this world was not the creation of Neo's mind. The truth is more sinister: the world was a creation of the artificially intelligent computers that have taken over the Earth and have subjugated mankind in the process. These creatures have fed Neo a simulation that he couldn't possibly help but take as the real thing. What's worse, it isn't clear how any of us can know with certainty that we are not in a position similar to Neo before his "rebirth." Our ordinary confidence in our ability to reason and our natural tendency to trust the deliverances of our senses can both come to seem rather naive once we confront this possibility of deception.

A viewer of *The Matrix* is naturally led to wonder: how do I know I am not in the Matrix? How do I know for sure that my world is not also a sophisticated charade, put forward by some super-human intelligence in such a way that I cannot possibly detect the ruse? The philosopher Rene Descartes suggested a similar worry: the frightening possibility that all of one's experiences might be the result of a powerful outside force, a "malicious demon."

"And yet firmly implanted in my mind is the long-standing opinion that there is an omnipotent God who made me the kind of creature that I am. How do I know that he has not brought it about that there is no earth, no sky, no extended thing, no shape, no size, no place, while at the same time ensuring that all these things appear to me to exist just as they do now? What is more, just as I consider that others sometimes go astray in cases where they think they have the most perfect knowledge, how do I know that God has not brought it about that I too go wrong every time I add two and three or count the sides of a square, or in some even simpler matter, if that is imaginable? But perhaps God would not have allowed me to be deceived in this way, since he is said to be supremely good; [...] I will suppose therefore that not God, who is supremely good and the source of truth, but rather some malicious demon of the utmost power and cunning has employed all his energies in order to deceive me. I shall think that the sky, the air, the earth, colours, shapes, sounds and all external things are merely the delusions of dreams which he has devised to ensnare my judgment." (*Meditations,* 15)

The narrator of Descartes' *Meditations* concludes that none of his former opinions are safe. Such a demon could not only deceive him about his perceptions, it could conceivably cause him to go wrong when performing even the simplest acts of reasoning.

This radical worry seems inescapable. How could you possibly prove to yourself that you are not in the kind of nightmarish situation Descartes describes? It would seem that any argument, evidence or proof you might put forward could easily be yet another trick played by the demon. As ludicrous as the idea of the evil demon may sound at first, it is hard, upon reflection, not to share Descartes' worry: for all you know, you may well be a mere plaything of such a malevolent intelligence. More to the point of our general discussion: for all you know, you may well be trapped in the Matrix.

Many contemporary philosophers have discussed a similar skeptical dilemma that is a bit closer to the scenario described in *The Matrix*. It has come to be known as the "brain in a vat" hypothesis, and one powerful formulation of the idea is presented by the philosopher Jonathan Dancy:

"You do not know that you are not a brain, suspended in a vat full of liquid in a laboratory, and wired to a computer which is feeding you your current experiences under the control of some ingenious technician scientist (benevolent or malevolent according to taste). For if you were such a brain, then, provided that the scientist is successful, nothing in your experience could possibly reveal that you were; for your experience is *ex hypothesi* identical with that of something which is not a brain in a vat. Since you have only your own experience to appeal to, and that experience is the same in either situation, nothing can reveal to you which situation is the actual one." (*Introduction to Contemporary Epistemology,* 10)

If you cannot know whether you are in the real world or in the word of a computer simulation, you cannot be sure that your beliefs about the world are true. And, what was even more frightening to Descartes, in this kind of scenario it seems that your ability to reason is no safer than the deliverances of the senses: the evil demon or malicious scientist could be ensuring that your reasoning is just as flawed as your perceptions.

As you have probably already guessed, there is no easy way out of this philosophical problem (or at least there is no easy *philosophical* way out!). Philosophers have proposed a dizzying variety of "solutions" to this kind of skepticism but, as with many philosophical problems, there is nothing close to unanimous agreement regarding how the puzzle should be solved.

Descartes' own way out of his evil demon skepticism was to first argue that one cannot genuinely doubt the existence of oneself. He pointed out that all thinking presupposes a thinker: even in doubting, you realize that there must at least be a self which is doing the doubting. (Thus Descartes' most famous line: "I think, therefore I am.") He then went on to claim that, in addition to our innate idea of self, each of us has an idea of God as an all-powerful, all-good, and infinite being implanted in our minds, and that this idea could only have come *from* God. Since this shows us that an all-good God does exist, we can have confidence that he would not allow us to be so drastically deceived about the nature of our perceptions and their relationship to reality. While Descartes' argument for the existence of the self has been tremendously influential and is still actively debated, few philosophers have followed him in accepting his particular theistic solution to skepticism about the external world.

One of the more interesting contemporary challenges to this kind of skeptical scenario has come from the philosopher Hilary Putnam. His point is not so much to defend our ordinary claims to knowledge as to question whether the "brain in a vat" hypothesis is coherent, given certain plausible assumptions about how our language refers to objects in the world. He asks us to consider a variation on the standard "brain in a vat" story that is uncannily similar to the situation described in *The Matrix*:

"Instead of having just one brain in a vat, we could imagine that all human beings (perhaps all sentient beings) are brains in a vat (or nervous systems in a vat in case some beings with just nervous systems count as 'sentient'). Of course, the evil scientist would have to be outside? or would he? Perhaps there is no evil scientist, perhaps (though this is absurd) the universe just happens to consist of automatic machinery tending a vat full of brains and nervous systems. This time let us suppose that the automatic machinery is programmed to give us all a *collective* hallucination, rather than a number of separate unrelated hallucinations. Thus, when I seem to myself to be talking to you, you seem to yourself to be hearing my words.... I want now to ask a question which will seem very silly and obvious (at least to some people, including some very sophisticated philosophers), but which will take us to real philosophical depths rather quickly. Suppose this whole story were actually true. Could we, if we were brains in a vat in this way, say or think that we were?" (*Reason, Truth, and History*, 7)

Putnam's surprising answer is that we cannot coherently think that we are brains in vats, and so skepticism of that kind can never really get off the ground. While it is difficult to do justice to Putnam's ingenious argument in a short summary, his point is roughly as follows:

Not everything that goes through our heads is a genuine thought, and far from everything we say is a meaningful utterance. Sometimes we get confused or think in an incoherent manner — sometimes we say things that are simply nonsense. Of course, we don't always realize at the time that we aren't making sense — sometimes we earnestly believe we are saying (or thinking) something meaningful. High on Nitrous Oxide, the philosopher William James was convinced he was having profound insights into the nature of reality — he was convinced that his thoughts were both sensical and important. Upon sobering up and looking at the notebook in which he had written his drug-addled thoughts, he saw only gibberish.

Just as I might say a sentence that is nonsense, I might also use a name or a general term which is meaningless in the sense that it fails to hook up to the world. Philosophers talk of such a term as "failing to refer" to an object. In order to successfully refer when we use language, there must be an appropriate relationship between the speaker and the object referred to. If a dog playing on the beach manages to scrawl the word "Ed" in the sand with a stick, few would want to claim that the dog actually meant to refer to someone named Ed. Presumably the dog doesn't know anyone named Ed, and even if he did, he wouldn't be capable of intending to write Ed's name in the sand. The point of such an example is that words do not refer to objects "magically" or intrinsically: certain conditions must be met in the world in order for us to accept that a given written or spoken word has any meaning and whether it actually refers to anything at all.

Putnam claims that one condition which is crucial for successful reference is that there be an appropriate causal connection between the object referred to and the speaker referring. Specifying exactly what should count as "appropriate" here is a notoriously difficult task, but we can get some idea of the kind of thing required by considering cases in which reference fails through an inappropriate connection: if someone unfamiliar with the film *The Matrix* manages to blurt out the word "Neo" while sneezing, few would be inclined to think that this person has actually *referred* to the character Neo. The kind of causal connection between the speaker and the object referred to (Neo) is just not in place. For reference to succeed, it can't be simply accidental that the name was uttered. (Another way to think about it: the sneezer would have uttered "Neo" even if the film *The Matrix* had never been made.)

The difficulty, according to Putnam, in coherently supposing the brain in a vat story to be true is that brains raised in such an environment could not successfully refer to genuine brains, or vats, or anything else in the real world. Consider the example of someone who has lived their entire life in the Matrix: when they talk of "chickens," they don't actually refer to real *chickens*; at best they refer to the computer representations of chickens that have been sent to their brain. Similarly, when they talk of human bodies being trapped in pods and fed data by the Matrix, they don't successfully refer to real bodies or pods — they can't refer to physical bodies in the real world because they cannot have the appropriate causal connection to such objects. Thus, if someone were to utter the sentence "I am simply a body stuck in a pod somewhere being fed sensory information by a computer" that sentence would itself be necessarily false. If the person is in fact not trapped in the Matrix, then the sentence is straightforwardly false. If the person is trapped in the Matrix, then he can't successfully refer to real human bodies when he utters the words "human body," and so it appears that his statement must also be false. Such a person seems thus doubly trapped: incapable of knowing that he is in the Matrix, and even incapable of successfully expressing the thought that he might be in the Matrix! (Could this be why at one point Morpheus tells Neo that "no one can be told what the Matrix is"?)

Putnam's argument is controversial, but it is noteworthy because it shows that the kind of situation described in *The Matrix* raises not just the expected philosophical issues about knowledge and skepticism, but more general issues regarding meaning, language, and the relationship between the mind and the world.

C. Cypher and the Experience Machine

Cypher is not a nice guy, but is he an unreasonable guy? Is he right to want to get re-inserted into the Matrix? Many want to say no, but giving reasons for why his choice is a bad one is not an easy task. After all, so long as his experiences will be pleasant, how can his situation be worse than the inevitably crappy life he would lead outside of the Matrix? What could matter beyond the quality of his experience? Remember, once he's back in, living his fantasy life, he won't even know he made the deal. What he doesn't know can't hurt him, right?

Is feeling good the only thing that has value in itself? The question of whether only conscious experience can ultimately matter is one that has been explored in depth by several contemporary philosophers. In the course of discussing this issue in his 1971 book *Anarchy, State, and Utopia* Robert Nozick introduced a "thought experiment" that has become a staple of introductory philosophy classes everywhere. It is known as "the experience machine":

"Suppose there were an experience machine that would give you any experience you desired. Superduper neuropsychologists could stimulate your brain so that you would think and feel you were writing a great novel, or making a friend, or reading an interesting book. All the time you would be floating in a tank, with electrodes attached to your brain. Should you plug into this machine for life, preprogramming your life's desires?...Of course, while in the tank you won't know that you're there; you'll think it's all actually happening. Others can also plug in to have the experiences they want, so there's no need to stay unplugged to serve them. (Ignore problems such as who will service the machines if everyone plugs in.) Would you plug in? What else can matter to us, other than how our lives feel from the inside?"

Nozick goes on to argue that other things do matter to us: For instance, that we actually do certain things, as opposed to simply have the experience of doing them. Also, he points out that we value being (and becoming) certain kinds of people. I don't just want to have the experience of being a decent person, I want to actually be a decent person. Finally, Nozick argues that we value contact with reality in itself, independent of any benefits such contact may bring through pleasant experience: we want to know we are experiencing the real thing. In sum, Nozick thinks that it matters to most of us, often in a rather deep way, that we be the authors of our lives and that our lives involve interacting with the world, and he thinks that the fact that most people would not choose to enter into such an experience machine demonstrates that they do value these other things. As he puts it: "We learn that something matters to us in addition to experience by imagining an experience machine and then realizing that we would not use it."

While Nozick's description of his machine is vague, it appears that there is at least one important difference between it and the simulated world of The Matrix. Nozick implies that someone hooked up to the experience machine will not be able exercise their agency — they become the passive recipients of preprogrammed experiences. This apparent loss of free will is disturbing to many people, and it might be distorting people's reactions to the case and clouding the issue of whether they value contact with reality per se. The Matrix seems to be set up in such a way that one can enter it and retain one's free will and capacity for decision making, and perhaps this makes it a significantly more attractive option than the experience machine Nozick describes.

Nonetheless, a loss of freedom is not the only disturbing aspect of Nozick's story. As he points out, we seem to mourn the loss of contact with the real world as well. Even if a modified experience machine is presented to us, one which allows us to keep our free will but enter into an entirely virtual world, many would still object that permanently going into such a machine involves the loss of something valuable.

Cypher and his philosophical comrades are likely to be unmoved by such observations. So what if most people are hung-up on "reality" and would turn down the offer to permanently enter an experience machine? Most people might be wrong. All their responses might show is that such people are superstitious, or irrational, or otherwise confused. Maybe they think something could go wrong with the machines, or maybe they keep forgetting that while in the machine they will no longer be aware of their choice to enter the machine.

Perhaps those hesitant to plug-in don't realize that they value being active in the real world only because normally that is the most reliable way for them to acquire the pleasant experience that they value in itself. In other words, perhaps our free will and our capacity to interact with reality are means to a further end — they matter to us because they allow us access to what really matters: pleasant conscious experience. To think the reverse, that reality and freedom have value in themselves (or what philosophers sometimes call non-derivative or intrinsic value), is simply to put the cart before the horse. After all, Cypher could reply, what would be so great about the capacity to freely make decisions or the ability to be in the real world if neither of these things allowed us to feel good?

Peter Unger has taken on these kinds of objections in his own discussion of "experience inducers". He acknowledges that there is a strong temptation when in a certain frame of mind to agree with this kind of Cypher-esque reasoning, but he argues that this is a temptation we ought to try and resist. Cypher's vision of value is too easy and too simplistic. We are inclined to think that only conscious experience can really matter in part because we fall into the grip of a particular picture of what values must be like, and this in turn leads us to stop paying attention to our actual values. We make ourselves blind to the subtlety and complexity of our values, and we then find it hard to understand how something that doesn't affect our consciousness could sensibly matter to us. If we stop and reflect on what we really do care about, however, we come across some surprisingly everyday examples that don't sit easily with Cypher's claims:

"Consider life insurance. To be sure, some among the insured may strongly believe that, if they die before their dependents do, they will still observe their beloved dependents, perhaps from a heaven on high. But others among the insured have no significant belief to that effect... Still, we all pay our premiums. In my case, this is because, even if I will never experience anything that happens to them, I still want things to go better, rather than worse, for my dependents. No doubt, I am rational in having this concern." (*Identity, Consciousness, and Value,* 301)

As Unger goes on to point out, it seems contrived to chalk up all examples of people purchasing life insurance to cases in which someone is simply trying to benefit (while alive) from the favorable impression such a purchase might make on the dependents. In many cases it seems ludicrous to deny that "what motivates us, of course, is our great concern for our dependent's future, whether we experience their future or not." This is not a proof that such concern is rational, but it does show that incidents in which we intrinsically value things other than our own conscious experience might be more widespread than we are at first liable to think. (Other examples include the value we place on not being deceived or lied to — the importance of this value doesn't seem to be completely exhausted by our concern that we might one day become aware of the lies and deception.)

Most of us care about a lot of things independently of the experiences that those things provide for us. The realization that we value things other than pleasant conscious experience should lead us to at least wonder if the legitimacy of this kind of value hasn't been too hastily dismissed by Cypher and his ilk. After all, once we see how widespread and commonplace our other non-derivative concerns are, the insistence that conscious experience is the only thing that has value in itself can come to seem downright peculiar. If purchasing life insurance seems like a rational thing to do, why shouldn't the desire that I experience reality (rather than some illusory simulation) be similarly rational? Perhaps the best test of the rationality of our most basic values is actually whether they, taken together, form a consistent and coherent network of attachments and concerns. (Do they make sense in light of each other and in light of our beliefs about the world and ourselves?) It isn't obvious that valuing interaction with the real world fails this kind of test.

Of course, pointing out that the value I place on living in the real world coheres well with my other values and beliefs will not quiet the defender of Cypher, as he will be quick to respond that the fact that my values all cohere doesn't show that they are all justified. Maybe I hold a bunch of exquisitely consistent but thoroughly irrational values!

The quest for some further justification of my basic values might be misguided, however. Explanations have to come to an end somewhere, as Ludwig Wittgenstein once famously remarked. Maybe the right response to a demand for justification here is to point out that the same demand can be made to Cypher: "Just what justifies your exclusive concern with pleasant conscious experience?" It seems as though nothing does — if such concern is justified it must be somehow self-justifying, but if that is possible, why shouldn't our concerns for other people and our desire to live in the real world also be self-justifying? If those can also be self-justifying, then maybe what we don't experience should matter to us, and perhaps what we don't know *can* hurt us...

Universe as a Numeric Simulation

1.INTRODUCTION

Extrapolations to the distant futurity of trends in the growth of high-performance computing (HPC) have led philosophers to question —in a logically compelling way— whether the universe that we currently inhabit is a numerical simulation performed by our distant descendants. With the current developments in HPC and in algorithms it is now possible to simulate Quantum Chromodynamics (QCD), the fundamental force in nature that gives rise to the strong nuclear force among protons and neutrons, and to nuclei and their interactions. These simulations are currently performed in femto-sized universes where the space-time continuum is replaced by a lattice, whose spatial and temporal sizes are of the order of several femtometers or fermis (1 fm = 10 −15 m), and whose lattice spacings (discretization or pixelation) are fractions of fermis 1 . This endeavor, generically referred to as lattice gauge theory, or more specifically lattice QCD, is currently leading to new insights into the nature of matter 2 . Within the next decade, with the anticipated deployment of exascale computing resources, it is expected that the nuclear forces will be determined from QCD, refining and extending their current determinations from experiment, enabling predictions for processes in extreme environments, or of exotic forms of matter, not accessible to laboratory experiments. Given the significant resources invested in determining the quantum fluctuations of the fundamental fields which permeate our universe, and in calculating nuclei from first principles it stands to reason that future simulation efforts will continue to extend to ever-smaller pixelations and ever-larger volumes of space-time, from the femto-scale to the atomic scale, and ultimately to macroscopic scales. If there are sufficient HPC resources available, then future scientists will likely make the effort to perform complete simulations of molecules, cells, humans and even beyond. Therefore, there is a sense in which lattice QCD may be viewed as the nascent science of universe simulation, and, as will be argued in the next paragraph, very basic extrapolation of current lattice QCD resource trends into the future suggest that experimental searches for evidence that our universe is, in fact, a simulation are both interesting and logical.

There is an extensive literature which explores various aspects of our universe as a simulation, from philosophical discussions, to considerations of the limits of computation within our own universe, to the inclusion of gravity and the standard model of particle physics into a quantum computation, and to the notion of our universe as a cellular automaton. There have also been extensive connections made between fundamental aspects of computation and physics, for example, the translation of the Church-Turing principle into the language of physicists by Deutsch. Finally, the observational consequences due to limitations in accuracy or flaws in a simulation have been considered . In this work, we take a pedestrian approach to the possibility that our universe is a simulation, by assuming that a classical computer (i.e. the classical limit of a quantum computer) is used to simulate the quantum universe (and its classical limit), as is done today on a very small scale, and ask if there are any signatures of this scenario that might be experimentally detectable.

Further, we do not consider the implications of, and constraints upon, the underlying information, and its movement, that are required to perform such extensive simulations. It is the case that the method of simulation, the algorithms, and the hardware that are used in future simulations are unknown, but it is conceivable that some of the ingredients used in present day simulations of quantum fields remain in use, or are used in other universes, and so we focus on one aspect only: the possibility that the simulations of the future employ an underlying cubic lattice structure.

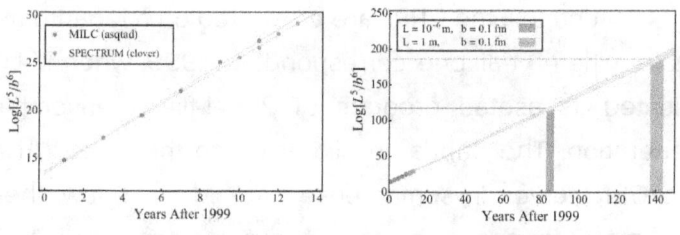

In contrast with Moore's law, which is a statement about the exponential growth of raw computing power in time, it is interesting to consider the historical growth of measures of the computational resource requirements (CRRs) of lattice QCD calculations, and extrapolations of this trend to the future. In order to do so, we consider two lattice generation programs: the MILC asqtad program , which over a twelve year span generated ensembles of lattice QCD gauge configurations, using the Kogut-Susskind (staggered) discretization of the quark fields, with lattice spacings, b, ranging from 0.18 to 0.045 fm, and lattice sizes (spatial extents), L, ranging from 2.5 to 5.8 fm, and the on-going anisotropic program carried out by the SPECTRUM collaboration, using the clover-Wilson discretization of the quark fields, which has generated lattice ensembles at b ~ 0.1 fm, with L ranging from 2.4 to 4.9 fm. At fixed quark masses, the CRR of a lattice ensemble generation (in units of petaFLOP-years) scales roughly as the dimensionless number λ QCD L 5/b 6 , where λ QCD $\equiv$ 1 fm is a typical QCD distance scale. In fig. 1 (left panel), the CRRs are presented on a logarithmic scale, where year one corresponds to 1999, when MILC initiated its asqtad program of 2 ı 1-flavor ensemble generation. The bands are linear fits to the data. While the CRR curves in some sense track Moore's law, they are more than a statement about increasing FLOPS. Since lattice QCD simulations include the quantum fluctuations of the vacuum and the effects of the strong nuclear force, the CRR curve is a statement about simulating universes with realistic fundamental forces. The extrapolations of the CRR trends into the future are shown in the right panel of fig. 1. The blue (red) horizontal

57

line corresponds to a lattice of the size of a micrometer (meter), a typical length scale of a cell (human), and at a lattice spacing of 0.1 fm. There are, of course, many caveats to this extrapolation. Foremost among them is the assumption that an effective Moore's Law will continue into the future, which requires technological and algorithmic developments to continue as they have for the past 40 years. Related to this is the possible existence of the technological singularity, which could alter the curve in unpredictable ways. And, of course, human extinction would terminate the exponential growth. However, barring such discontinuities in the curve, these estimates are likely to be conservative as they correspond to full simulations with the fundamental forces of nature. With finite resources at their disposal, our descendants will likely make use of effective theory methods, as is done today, to simulate every-increasing complexity, by, for instance, using meshes that adapt to the relevant physical length scales, or by using fluid dynamics to determine the behavior of fluids, which are constrained to rigorously reproduce the fundamental laws of nature. Nevertheless, one should keep in mind that the CRR curve is based on lattice QCD ensemble generation and therefore is indicative of the ability to simulate the quantum fluctuations associated with the fundamental forces of nature at a given lattice spacing and size. The cost to perform the measurements that would have to be done in the background of these fluctuations in order to simulate —for instance— a cell could, in principle, lie on a significantly steeper curve.

We should comment on the simulation scenario in the context of ongoing attempts to discover the theoretical structure that underlies the Standard Model of particle physics, and the expectation of the unification of the forces of nature at very short distances. There has not been much interest in the notion of an underlying lattice structure of space-time for several reasons. Primary among them is that in Minkowski space, a non-vanishing spatial lattice spacing generically breaks space-time symmetries in such a way that there are dimension-four Lorentz breaking operators in the Standard Model, requiring a large number of fine-tunings to restore Lorentz invariance to experimentally verified levels. The fear is that even though Lorentz violating dimension four operators can be tuned away at tree-level, radiative corrections will induce them back at the quantum level as is discussed in Refs.. This is not an issue if one assumes the simulation scenario for the same reason that it is not an issue when one performs a lattice QCD calculation 3 . The underlying space-time symmetries respected by the lattice action will necessarily be preserved at the quantum level. In addition, the notion of a simulated universe is sharply at odds with the reductionist prejudice in particle physics which suggests the unification of forces with a simple and beautiful predictive mathematical description at very short distances. However, the discovery of the string landscape], and the current inability of string theory to provide a useful predictive framework which would post-dict the fundamental parameters of the Standard Model, provides the simulators (future string theorists?) with a purpose: to systematically explore the landscape of vacua through numerical simulation. If it is indeed the case that the fundamental equations of nature allow on the order of 10 500 solutions, then perhaps the most profound quest that can be undertaken by a sentient being is the exploration of the landscape through universe simulation. In some weak sense, this exploration is already underway with current investigations of a class of confining beyond-the-Standard- Model (BSM) theories, where there is only minimal experimental guidance at present (for one recent example, see Ref. [31]). Finally, one may be tempted to view lattice gauge theory as a primitive numerical tool, and that the simulator should be expected to have more efficient ways of simulating reality. However, one should keep in mind that the only known way to define QCD as a consistent quantum field theory is in the context of lattice QCD, which suggests a fundamental role for the lattice formulation of gauge theory.

Physicists, in contrast with philosophers, are interested in determining observable consequences of the hypothesis that we are a simulation 4 5 . In lattice QCD, space-time is replaced by a finite hyper-cubic grid of points over which the fields are defined, and the (now) finite-dimensional quantum mechanical path integral is evaluated. The grid breaks Lorentz symmetry (and hence rotational symmetry), and its effects have been defined within the context of a low-energy effective field theory (EFT), the Symanzik action, when the lattice spacing is small compared with any physical length scales in the problem. The lattice action can be modified to systematically improve calculations of observables, by adding irrelevant operators with coefficients that can be determined non perturbatively. For instance, the Wilson action can be O(b)-improved by including the Sheikholeslami-Wohlert term. Given this low-energy description, we would like to investigate the hypothesis that we are a simulation with the assumption that the development of simulations of the universe in some sense parallels the development of lattice QCD calculations. That is, early simulations use the computationally "cheapest" discretizations with no improvement. In particular, we will assume that the simulation of our universe is done on a hyper-cubic grid 7 and, as a starting point, we will assume that the simulator is using an unimproved Wilson action, that produces O(b) artifacts of the form of the Sheikholeslami-Wohlert operator inthe low-energy theory 8 .

2. UNIMPROVED WILSON SIMULATION OF THE UNIVERSE

The simplest gauge invariant action of fermions which does not contain doublers is the Wilson action,

$$
S^{(W)} = b^4 \sum_x \mathcal{L}^{(W)}(x) = b^4 \left(m + \frac{4}{b} \right) \sum_x \bar{\psi}(x)\psi(x)
$$
$$
+ \frac{b^3}{2} \sum_x \bar{\psi}(x) \left[(\gamma_\mu - 1) \ U_\mu(x) \ \psi(x + b\hat{\mu}) - (\gamma_\mu + 1) \ U_\mu^\dagger(x - b\hat{\mu}) \ \psi(x - b\hat{\mu}) \right]
$$

which describes a fermion, ψ, of mass m interacting with a gauge field, A μ (x), through the gauge link,

$$
U_\mu(x) = \exp \left(ig \int_x^{x+b\hat{\mu}} dz A_\mu(z) \right)
$$

where $\hat{\mu}$ is a unit vector in the μ-direction, and g is the coupling constant of the theory. Expanding the Lagrangian density, L (W), in the lattice spacing (that is small compared with the physical length scales), and performing a field redefinition, it can be shown that the Lagrangian density takes the form

$$\mathcal{L}^{(W)} = \overline{\psi}\slashed{D}\psi \; + \; \tilde{m}\overline{\psi}\psi \; + \; C_p \frac{gb}{4}\overline{\psi}\sigma_{\mu\nu}G^{\mu\nu}\psi \; + \; \mathcal{O}(b^2),$$

where G μν = −i[D μ , D ν]/g is the field strength tensor and D μ is the covariant derivative. M̃ is a redefined mass which contains O(b) lattice spacing artifacts (that can be tuned away). The coefficient of the Pauli term ψσ μν G μν ψ is fixed at tree level, C p = 1 + O(α), where α = g 2 /(4π). It is worth noting that as is usual in lattice QCD calculations, the lattice action can be O(b) improved by adding a term of the form δL (W) = C sw gb ψσ μν G μν ψ to the 4 Lagrangian with C sw = −C p + O(α). This is the so-called Sheikholeslami-Wohlert term. Of course there is no reason to assume that the simulator had to have performed such an improvement in simulating the universe.

3. ROTATIONALLY INVARIANT MODIFICATIONS

Lorentz symmetry is recovered in lattice calculations as the lattice spacing vanishes when compared with the scales of the system. It is useful to consider contributions to observables from a non-zero lattice spacing that are Lorentz invariant and consequently rotationally invariant, and those that are not. While the former type of modifications could arise from many different BSM scenarios, the latter, particularly modifications that exhibit cubic symmetry, would be suggestive of a structure consistent with an underlying discretization of space-time.

1. QED Fine Structure Constant and the Anomalous Magnetic Moment

For our present purposes, we will assume that Quantum Electrodynamics (QED) is simulated with this unimproved action, eq. (1). The $O(b)$ contribution to the lattice action induces an additional contribution to the fermion magnetic moments. Specifically, the Lagrange density that describes electromagnetic interactions is given by eq. (3), where the interaction with an external magnetic field B is described through the covariant derivative $D_\mu = \partial_\mu + ie\hat{Q}A_\mu$ with $e > 0$ and the electromagnetic charge operator $\hat{Q}$, and where the vector potential satisfies $\nabla \times$

A = B. The interaction Hamiltonian density in Minkowski-space is given by

$$\mathcal{H}_{int} = \frac{e}{2m}\bar{\psi}A_\mu(i\overrightarrow{\partial}^\mu - i\overleftarrow{\partial}^\mu)\hat{Q}\psi \; + \; \frac{\hat{Q}e}{4m}\bar{\psi}\sigma_{\mu\nu}F^{\mu\nu}\psi \; + \; C_p\frac{\hat{Q}eb}{4}\bar{\psi}\sigma_{\mu\nu}F^{\mu\nu}\psi \; + \; ... \; .$$

where $F\mu\nu = \partial\mu A\nu - \partial\nu A\mu$ is the electromagnetic field strength tensor, and the ellipses denote terms suppressed by additional powers of b. By performing a non-relativistic reduction, the last two terms in eq. 4 give rise to H int,mag = −μ · B, where the electron magnetic moment μ is given by

$$\boldsymbol{\mu} = \frac{\hat{Q}e}{2m}\left(g + 2mb\,C_p + ...\right)\boldsymbol{S} \; = \; g(b)\frac{\hat{Q}e}{2m}\,\boldsymbol{S} \; .$$

where g is the usual fermion g-factor and S is its spin. Note that the lattice spacing contribution to the magnetic moment is enhanced relative to the Dirac contribution by one power of the particle mass.

For the electron, the effective g-factor has an expansion at finite lattice spacing of

$$\frac{g^{(e)}(b)}{2} = 1 + C_2\left(\frac{\alpha}{\pi}\right) + C_4\left(\frac{\alpha}{\pi}\right)^2 + C_6\left(\frac{\alpha}{\pi}\right)^3 + C_8\left(\frac{\alpha}{\pi}\right)^4 + C_{10}\left(\frac{\alpha}{\pi}\right)^5$$
$$+ \; a_{\mathrm{hadrons}} \; + \; a_{\mu,\tau} \; + \; a_{\mathrm{weak}} \; + \; m_e b\,C_p \; + \; ... \; ,$$

where the coefficients C i , in general, depend upon the ratio of lepton masses. The calculation (e) by Schwinger provides the leading coefficient of C 2 = 12 . The experimental value of g expt /2 = 1.001 159 652 180 73(28) gives rise to the best determination of the fine structure constant α (at b = 0) [39]. However, when the lattice spacing is non-zero, the extracted value of α becomes a function of b,

$$\alpha(b) = \alpha(0) \; - \; 2\pi m_e b \, \mathcal{C}_p \; + \; \mathcal{O}\left(\alpha^2 b\right)$$

where α(0) −1 = 137.035 999 084(51) is determined from the experimental value of electron g-factor as quoted above. With one experimental constraint and two parameters to determine, α and b, unique values for these quantities cannot be established, and an orthogonal constraint is required. One can look at the muon g − 2 which has a similar QED expansion to that of the electron, including the contribution from the non-zero lattice spacing,

$$\frac{g^{(\mu)}(b)}{2} = 1 + C_2^{(\mu)}\left(\frac{\alpha}{\pi}\right) + C_4^{(\mu)}\left(\frac{\alpha}{\pi}\right)^2 + C_6^{(\mu)}\left(\frac{\alpha}{\pi}\right)^3 + C_8^{(\mu)}\left(\frac{\alpha}{\pi}\right)^4 + C_{10}^{(\mu)}\left(\frac{\alpha}{\pi}\right)^5$$
$$+ \, a_{\text{hadrons}}^{(\mu)} \; + \; a_{e,\tau}^{(\mu)} \; + \; a_{\text{weak}}^{(\mu)} \; + \; m_\mu b \, \mathcal{C}_p \; + \; ... \quad .$$

Inserting the electron g − 2 (at finite lattice spacing) gives

$$\frac{g^{(\mu)}(b)}{2} = \frac{g^{(\mu)}(0)}{2} + (m_\mu - m_e)b\, C_p + \mathcal{O}\left(\alpha^2 b\right)$$

Given that the standard model calculation of g (μ) (0) is consistent with the experimental value, with a ~ 3.6σ deviation, one can put a limit on b from the difference and uncertainty in theoretical and experimental values of g (μ) , g expt /2 = 1.001 165 920 89(54)(33) and (μ) g theory /2 = 1.001 165 918 02(2)(42)(26). Attributing this difference to a finite lattice spacing, these values give rise to

b −1 = (3.6 ± 1.1) × 10 7 GeV ,

which provides an approximate upper bound on the lattice spacing.

2. The Rydberg Constant and α

Another limit can be placed on the lattice spacing from differences between the value of α extracted from the electron g −2 and from the Rydberg constant, R ∞ . The latter extraction, as discussed in Ref. [39], is rather complicated, with the value of the R ∞ obtained from a χ 2 - minimization fit involving the experimentally determined energy-level splittings. However, to recover the constraints on the Dirac energy-eigenvalues (which

67

then lead to R_∞), theoretical corrections must be first removed from the experimental values. To begin with, one can obtain an estimate for the limit on b by considering the differences between a's obtained from various methods assuming that the only contributions are from QED and the lattice spacing. Given that it is the reduced mass ($\mu \sim m_e$) that will compensate the lattice spacing in these QED determinations (for an atom at rest in the lattice frame), one can write

$$\delta a = 2\pi m_e b \tilde{C}_p$$

where $\tilde{C}_p$ is a number O(1) by naive dimensional analysis, and is a combination of the contributions from the two independent extractions of a. There is no reason to expect complete cancellation between the contributions from two different extractions. In fact, it is straightforward to show that the O(b) contribution to the value of a determined from the Rydberg constant is suppressed by $a^4 m_e^2$, and therefore the above assumption is robust. In addition to the electron g − 2 determination of fine structure constant as quoted above, the next precise determination of a comes form the atomic recoil experiments, $a^{-1} = 137.035\ 999\ 049(90)\ 9$, given an a priori determined value of the Rydberg constant. This gives rise to a difference of $|\delta a| =$

$(1.86 \pm 5.51) \times 10^{-12}$ between two extractions, which translates into

$$b = | (-0.6 \pm 1.7) \times 10^{-9} | \ GeV^{-1}$$

As this result is consistent with zero, the 1σ values of the lattice spacing give rise to a limit of

$$b^{-1} > 4 \times 10^{8} \ GeV \ ,$$

which is seen to be an order of magnitude more precise than that arising from the muon $g - 2$.

For more sophisticated simulations in which chiral symmetry is preserved by the lattice discretization, the coefficient C_p will vanish or will be exponentially small. As a result, the bound on the lattice spacing derived from the muon $g - 2$ and from the differences between determinations of α will be significantly weaker. In these analyses, we have worked with QED only, and have not included the full electroweak interactions as chiral gauge theories have not yet been successfully latticized. Consequently, these constraints are to be considered estimates only, and a more complete analysis needs to be performed when chiral gauge theories can be simulated.

4. ROTATIONAL SYMMETRY BREAKING

While there are more conventional scenarios for BSM physics that generate deviations in g−2 from the standard model prediction, or differences between independent determinations of α, the breaking of rotational symmetry would be a solid indicator of an underlying space-time grid, although not the only one. As has been extensively discussed in the literature, another scenario that gives rise to rotational invariance violation involves the introduction of an external background with a preferred direction. Such a preferred direction can be defined via a fixed vector, u_μ. The effective low-energy Lagrangian of such a theory contains Lorentz covariant higher dimension operators with a coupling to this background vector, and breaks both parity and Lorentz invariance. Dimension three, four and five operators, however, are shown to be severely constrained by experiment, and such contributions in the low-energy action (up to dimension five) have been ruled out.

3. Atomic Level Splittings

At $O(b^2)$ in the lattice spacing expansion of the Wilson action, that is relevant to describing low-energy processes, there is a rotational-symmetry breaking

70

operator that is consistent with the lattice hyper-cubic symmetry,

$$\mathcal{L}^{RV} = C^{RV} \frac{b^2}{6} \sum_{\mu=1}^{4} \overline{\psi} \, \gamma_\mu D_\mu D_\mu D_\mu \, \psi$$

where the tree-level value of C RV = 1. In taking matrix elements of this operator in the Hydrogen atom, where the binding energy is suppressed by a factor of α compared with the typical momentum, the dominant contribution is from the spatial components. As each spatial momentum scales as m e α, in the non-relativistic limit, shifts in the energy levels are expected to be of order

$$\delta E \sim C^{RV} \alpha^4 m_e^3 b^2$$

To understand the size of energy splittings, a lattice spacing of b −1 = 10 8 GeV gives an energy shift of order δE ~ 10 −26 eV, including for the splittings between substates in given irreducible representations of SO(3) with angular momentum J ≥ 2. This magnitude of energy shifts and splittings is presently unobservable. Given present technology, and constraints imposed on the lattice spacing by other observables, we conclude that there is little chance to see such an effect in the atomic spectrum.

4. The Energy-Momentum Relation and Cosmic Rays

Constraints on Lorentz-violating perturbations to the standard model of electroweak interactions from differences in the maximal attainable velocity (MAV) of particles, and on interactions with a non-zero vector field , have been determined previously. Assuming that each particle satisfies an energy-momentum relation of the form $E_i^2 = |p_i|^2 c_i^2 + m_i^2 c_i^4$ (along with the conservation of both energy and momentum in any given process), if c_γ exceeds $c_{e\pm}$, the process $\gamma \to e^+ e^-$ becomes possible for photons with an energy greater than the critical energy $E_{crit.} = 2 m_e c^2 e c_\gamma / \sqrt{(c_\gamma^2 - c_{e\pm}^2)}$ and the observation of high energy primary cosmic photons with $E_\gamma \le 20\,\mathrm{TeV}$ translates into the constraint $c_\gamma - c_{e\pm} \le 10^{15}$ presents a series of exceedingly tight constraints on differences between the speed of light between different particles, with typical sizes of $\delta c_{ij} \le 10^{-21} - 10^{-22}$

72

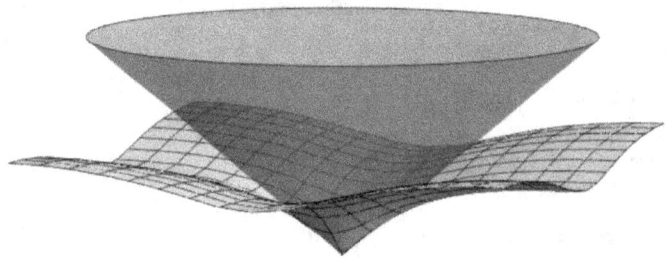

FIG. 2. The energy surface of a massless, non-interacting Wilson fermion with r = 1 as a function of momentum in the x and y directions, bounded by $-\pi < bp_{x,y} < \pi$, for p_z = 0 is shown in blue. The continuum dispersion relation is shown as the red surface.

for particles of species i and j. At first glance, these constraints would appear to also provide tight constraints on the size of the lattice spacing used in a simulation of the universe. However, this is not the case. As the speed of light for each particle in the discretized space-time depends on its three-momentum, the constraints obtained by Coleman and Glashow do not directly apply to processes occurring in a lattice simulation.

The dispersion relations satisfied by bosons and Wilson fermions in a lattice simulation (in Minkowski space) are

$$\sinh^2(\frac{bE_b}{2}) - \sum_{j=1,2,3} \sin^2(\frac{bk_j}{2}) - (\frac{bm_b}{2})^2 = 0 \; ;$$

$$E_b = \sqrt{|\mathbf{k}|^2 + m_b^2} + \mathcal{O}(b^2) \quad ,$$

and

$$\sinh^2(bE_f) - \sum_{j=1,2,3} \sin^2(bk_j) - \left[bm_f + 2r \left(\sum_{j=1,2,3} \sin^2(\frac{bk_j}{2}) - \sinh^2(\frac{bE_f}{2}) \right) \right]^2 = 0$$

$$E_f = \sqrt{|\mathbf{k}|^2 + m_f^2} - \frac{r \, b \, m_f^3}{2\sqrt{|\mathbf{k}|^2 + m_f^2}} + \mathcal{O}(b^2) \quad ,$$

respectively, where r is the coefficient of the Wilson term, E b and E f are the energy of a boson and fermion with momentum k, respectively. The summations are performed over the components along the lattice Cartesian axes corresponding to the x,y, and z spatial directions. The implications of these dispersion relations for neutrino oscillations along one of the lattice axes have been considered in Ref. [46]. Further, they have been considered as a possible explanation of the (now retracted) OPERA result suggesting superluminal neutrinos. The violation of Lorentz invariance resulting from these dispersion relations is due to the fact that they have only cubic symmetry and not full rotational symmetry, as shown in fig. 2. It is in the limit of small momentum, compared to the inverse lattice spacing, that the dispersion relations exhibit rotational invariance. While for the fundamental particles, the dispersion relations in eq. (16) and eq. (17) are valid, for composite particles, such as the proton or pion, the dispersion relations will be dynamically generated. In the present analysis we assume that the dispersion relations for all particles take the form of those in eq. (16) and eq. (17). It is also interesting to note that the polarizations of the massless vector fields are not exactly perpendicular to their direction of propagation for some directions of propagation with respect to the lattice axes, with longitudinal components present for non-zero lattice spacings.

Consider the process $p \rightarrow p + \gamma$, which is forbidden in the vacuum by energy-momentum conservation in special relativity when the speed of light of the proton and photon are equal, $c_p = c_\gamma$. Such a process can proceed in-medium when $v_p > c_\gamma$, corresponding to Cerenkov radiation. In the situation where the proton and photon have different MAV's, the absence. In lattice simulations of this process in vacuum requires that $|c_p - c_\gamma| \sim 10^{-23}$ the universe, this process could proceed in the vacuum if there are final state momenta which satisfy energy conservation for an initial state proton with energy E_i moving in some direction with respect to the underlying cubic lattice. Numerically, we find that there are no final states that satisfy this condition, and therefore this process is forbidden for all proton momentum 10 . In contrast, the process $\gamma \rightarrow e + e-$, which provides tight constraints on differences between MAV's , can proceed for very high energy photons (those with energies comparable to the inverse lattice spacing) near the edges of the Brillouin zone. Further, very high energy $\pi 0$'s are stable against $\pi 0 \rightarrow \gamma\gamma$, as is the related process $\gamma \rightarrow \pi 0 \gamma$.

With the dispersion relation of special relativity, the structure of the cosmic ray spectrum is greatly impacted by the inelastic collisions of nucleons with the cosmic microwave background (CMB) [50, 51]. Processes such as $\gamma CMB + N \rightarrow \Delta$ give rise to the predicted GKZ-cut off scale [50, 51] of $\sim 6\times10$ 20 eV in the spectrum of high energy cosmic rays. Recent experimental observations show a decline in the fluxes starting around this value [52, 53], indicating that the GKZ-cut off (or some other cut off mechanism) is present in the cosmic ray flux. For lattice spacings corresponding to an energy scale comparable to the GKZ cut off, the cosmic ray spectrum will exhibit significant deviations from isotropy, revealing the cubic structure of the lattice. However, for lattice spacings much smaller than the GKZ cut off scale, the GKZ mechanism cuts off the spectrum, effectively hiding the underlying lattice structure. When the lattice rest frame coincides with the CMB rest frame, head-on interactions between a high energy proton with momentum |p| and a photon of (very-low) energy ω can proceed through the Δ resonance when

$$\omega = \frac{m_\Delta^2 - m_N^2}{4|\mathbf{p}|} \left[1 + \frac{\sqrt{\pi}b^2|\mathbf{p}|^2}{9} \left(Y_4^0(\theta,\phi) + \sqrt{\frac{5}{14}} \left(Y_4^{+4}(\theta,\phi) + Y_4^{-4}(\theta,\phi) \right) \right) \right]$$
$$- \frac{m_\Delta^3 - m_N^3}{4|\mathbf{p}|} br + \cdots ,$$

for |p| 1/b, where θ and φ are the polar and azimuthal angles of the particle momenta in the rest frame of the lattice, respectively. This represents a lower bound for the energy of photons participating in such a process with arbitrary collision angles.

The lattice spacing itself introduces a cut off to the cosmic ray spectrum. For both the fermions and the bosons, the cut off from the dispersion relation is E max ~ 1/b. Equating this to the GKZ cut off corresponds to a lattice spacing of b ~ 10 −12 fm, or a mass scale of b 1 10 11 GeV. Therefore, the lattice spacing used in the lattice simulation of the universe must be b<10^-12 fm in order for the GZK cut off to be present or for the lattice spacing itself to provide the cut off in the cosmic ray spectrum. The most striking feature of the scenario in which the lattice provides the cut off to the cosmic ray spectrum is that the angular distribution of the highest energy components would exhibit cubic symmetry in the rest frame of the lattice, deviating significantly from isotropy. For smaller lattice spacings, the cubic distribution would be less significant, and the GKZ mechanism would increasingly dominate the high energy structure. It may be the case that more advanced simulations will be performed with non-cubic lattices. The results obtained for cubic lattices indicate that the symmetries of the non-cubic lattices should be imprinted, at some level, on the high energy cosmic ray spectrum.

In this work, we have taken seriously the possibility that our universe is a numerical simulation. In particular, we have explored a number of observables that may reveal the underlying structure of a simulation performed with a rigid hyper-cubic space-time grid. This is motivated by the progress in performing lattice QCD calculations involving the fundamental fields and interactions of nature in femto-sized volumes of space-time, and by the simulation hypothesis of Bostrom . A number of elements required for a simulation of our universe directly from the fundamental laws of physics have not yet been established, and we have assumed that they will, in fact, be developed at some point in the future; two important elements being an algorithm for simulating chiral gauge theories, and quantum gravity. It is interesting to note that in the simulation scenario, the fundamental energy scale defined by the lattice spacing can be orders of magnitude smaller than the Planck scale, in which case the conflict between quantum mechanics and gravity should be absent.

The spectrum of the highest energy cosmic rays provides the most stringent constraint that we have found on the lattice spacing of a universe simulation, but precision measurements, particularly the muon $g - 2$, are within a few orders of magnitude of being sensitive to the chiral symmetry breaking aspects of a simulation employing the unimproved Wilson lattice action. Given the ease with which current lattice QCD simulations incorporate improvement or employ discretizations that preserve chiral symmetry, it seems unlikely that any but the very earliest universe simulations would be unimproved with respect to the lattice spacing. Of course, improvement in this context masks much of our ability to probe the possibility that our universe is a simulation, and we have seen that, with the exception of the modifications to the dispersion relation and the associated maximum values of energy and momentum, even $O(b^2)$ operators in the Symanzik action easily avoid obvious experimental probes. Nevertheless, assuming that the universe is finite and therefore the resources of potential simulators are finite, then a volume containing a simulation will be finite and a lattice spacing must be non-zero, and therefore in principle there always remains the possibility for the simulated to discover the simulators.

Is this a video Game?

Recently, the idea that we may be living in a giant video game, or as it's sometimes called, *the Simulation Hypothesis*, has gotten a lot of attention because of prominent figures like Elon Musk who have openly discussed the idea. As Virtual Reality technology has gotten more sophisticated, we are starting to contemplate virtual worlds like that of the omni-present *Oasis* in *Ready Player One*, soon to be a blockbuster movie directed by Steven Spielberg.

Some like sci fi writer Philip K. Dick, believed strongly that we were living in a kind of simulation. Others, like futurist Ray Kurzweil, have popularized the idea of downloading our consciousness into a silicon based device, which would mean we are just digital information after all. Some, like Oxford lecturer Nick Bostrom, goes further and thinks we may in fact be artificially simulated consciousness inside such a simulation already!

Science Fiction Or Mysticism?

Like my first exposure to most great ideas, I discovered the Simulation Hypothesis through watching and reading too much science fiction.

The first time was during an episode of *Star Trek: The Next Generation*, where a holodeck character realized that he was in a simulation and that some of the people in the simulation existed "out there" (in this case, *out there* was the rest of the Enterprise) and he wanted to go there, too! Was it possible that we were in a "holodeck-like" space and that there was another world "out there", I wondered?

A Star Trek character in the Holodeck realizes that he is in a simulation

Although this was only a passing thought at the time, it wasn't until the movie *the Matrix* was released in 1999 that the idea grew in the popular consciousness. It occurred to me then that this kind of simulation could exist with or without the overlords that make this a nightmare scenario (in both *the Matrix* and Elon Musk's version of the giant video game, there are super-intelligent overlords behind the simulation, in one case evolved machines and in another aliens!).

The Matrix planted the idea in the popular consciousness that we are in a simulated reality

As a computer scientist and video game designer, I have to admit that this idea is not really that crazy. A civilization that implemented an advanced simulation like ours might be many thousands (even *millions*) of years ahead of us; it's not that hard to imagine such a civilization creating much more sophisticated games than we are capable of building today.

As I started to study Quantum Physics and its startling revelations about the nature of "objective" vs. "subjective" reality, I started to wonder again about the idea of a giant multiplayer video game. Moreover, as I delved more into the Eastern traditions, particularly Yogic and Buddhist philosophy, I found that their ideas about the nature of the world were actually pretty consistent with the idea that we are living in a simulation.

Why Might This Be A Video Game After All

Let's delve into the top reasons why we may be living in a simulation after all:

1. Pixels, Resolution, Virtual and Augmented Reality

One of the main arguments that Musk makes is that a more advanced civilization will have games that are of very high resolution—so high that we would be unable to distinguish between the "real" world and a "simulated one".

Today we are already seeing with Virtual Reality that "full immersion" is possible. Anyone who has played a convincing VR game will realize that it's possible to forget about the real world and "believe" the world you are seeing is real.

As a great example, I was playing a prototype of a Ping Pong VR game last year (built by Free Range Games), and even though it wasn't realistic resolution, I lost myself and thought I was playing ping pong for real. So much so that I set the paddle on the ping pong "table" and leaned against the table. Of course it was a VR table so it didn't really exist—I ended up dropping the paddle (actually the Vive controller) onto the floor. As I leaned into the "table" I almost fell over before realizing that *there was no table*. In other words, *to quote from the Matrix, there is no spoon.*

In Ready Player One, a realistic immersive virtual reality world, Oasis, becomes the ultimate escape

Imaging what kind of pixel resolution we might have in a hundred years, let alone in *a thousand years*! It could be pretty convincing. Also, as AR technology evolves to project onto the retina without needing external glasses, we could be seeing things around us that aren't really there in a resolution that's indistinguishable from the physical world. This brings up the idea that the world "out there" could really be just a projection in our minds.

2. Pixels, Quanta, and Xeno's Paradox.

I recall late nights at college during my undergrad years where I had philosophical debates with my classmates about the nature of reality. This was the first time I'd heard of Xeno's paradox. The idea was that if space was continuous, like numbers are (you can always find an infinite number of numbers in between any two numbers), how is it possible to touch an object such as the wall? You would always have to cover half the distance and neve get there.

Xeno (or Zeno, whichever spelling you prefer!) related the paradox using the example of Achilles and a tortoise. If the tortoise was ahead of Achilles, how could he possibly ever catch it if he always had to make up "half the distance"?

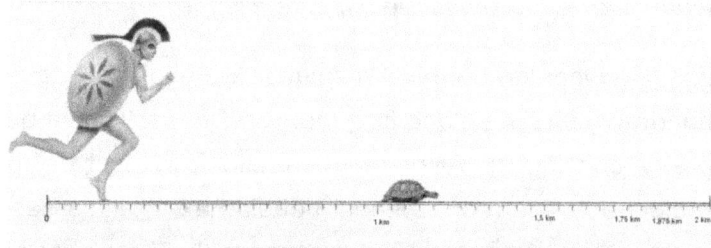

When I first heard about this paradox, my initial reaction was that space must be quantized—there must be some minimum distance that we traverse. Later, I discovered that I wasn't alone in this idea; whether this "minimum" amount is the Planck constant or some other amount isn't as important as the idea that the physical universe, as we know it, may consists of pixels. Just like a video game! How many pixels are in the real world? To use a non-scientific term, a shitload.

3. An Open World and the Illusion of Infinite Possibilities.

Early video games were very linearly structured, such as space invaders or Pac-Man. There was a limited set of "motions" that were allowable using some "input" control, and there were specific objective as part of the each level, and you progressed linearly through the levels.

As video games evolved and 3d models of a "world" became commonplace, video games took an evolutionary leap. It seemed from the player's perspective that you could move around and do anything. Examples of open world video games range from *GTA* (Grand Theft Auto) and *WOW* (World of Warcraft), or *the Sims*, which simulated life and eventually

Virtual Worlds like *Second Life*. Of course the idea that he world is infinite and that we can do "anything" inside the world is a carefully crafted illusion.

Game designers know that's not true. Using 3D modeling we can have a world that is generated and looks infinite but is really a set of maps and rules. In any game, no matter how "open" it appears, there are underlying tasks, or quests, or accomplishments, which are mapped out by the game designers. Is it possible that we have a similar illusion of "openness" in life?

Open World games like Second Life give the illusion of free choice

4. The Collapse of the Probability Wave, Future Selves, and Parallel Universes

In Quantum physics one of the most intriguing ideas is the probability matrix, which is an interpretation of how subatomic particles can exhibit properties of *both* a wave *and* a solid particle at the same time. At the level of an electron or a photon, the wave is interpreted as a set of probabilities of where the particle might be at any given time. When we observe a particular possibility, then the probability wave is said to "collapse" and we see a single particle in a particular location.

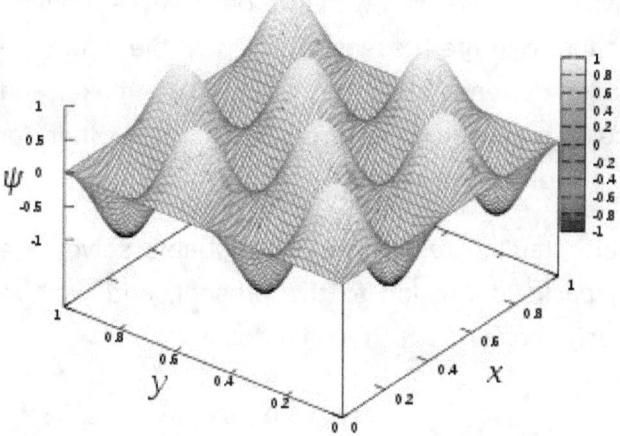

Probability wave of the location of a particle

Some interpreters have taken this to the macro level to say that there are a set of probabilities in which we exist both in the present and in the future.

Which of the possible paths do we follow? There isn't a good explanation; how the probability wave collapses is one of the biggest mysteries in Quantum Physics. The best answer physicists have come up with is that *consciousness* somehow determines the collapse.

Physicist Fred Alan Wolf, for example, says that information from these possible futures is coming to us in the present and that we send out an "offer wave" into the future, which is interacting with the "offer waves" coming from the future to the present. Which possible future we navigate to depends on which choices we make, and how these two waves superpose on each other (or cancel each other out).

These are startling results. Future probable selves are sending back information to the present, and we are consciously choosing which path to follow.

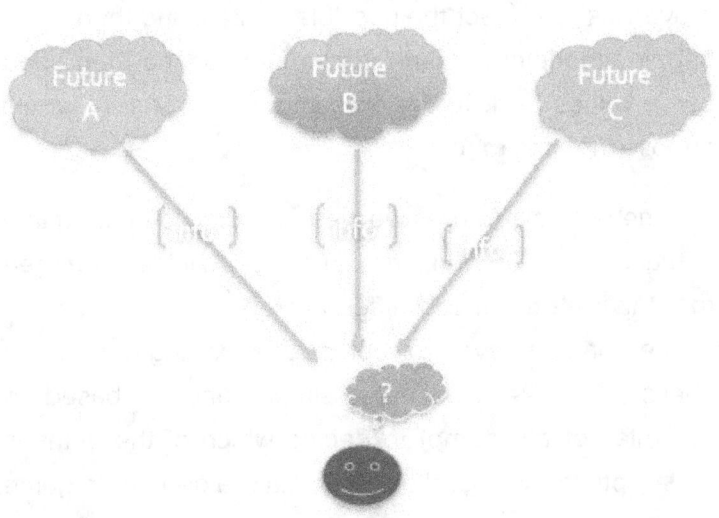

Figure 1: Multiple Probable Futures Are Sending Us Back Information we use to make decisions.

Another related aspect of Quantum Physics that sounds like science fiction is the Parallel Universes theory, where we branch into different "universes" when we make decisions. If that's true, then there is a directed graph of multiple universes that are branching out each time we make a decision, resulting in different timelines (in fact, the parallel universes theory was put forward to solve the grandfather paradox of time travel).

This reminded me of the very first video game I made back at MIT. The way that the computer chose the next move was to project the possible futures, and then use a certain algorithm to "rank" those futures, and then bring those values back to the present and then the AI would choose the path to follow.

Did the possible futures we were calculating in our game actually exist? Or were they just probabilities? I realized that this isn't too much different from what's happening at the quantum level, except that in existing games like chess or checkers, we use a simple function (based on the rules of the game) to decide which of the paths is most optimal. We used the "minimax" algorithm in game design, trying to maximize our score and minimize our opponents score at each "turn of the future".

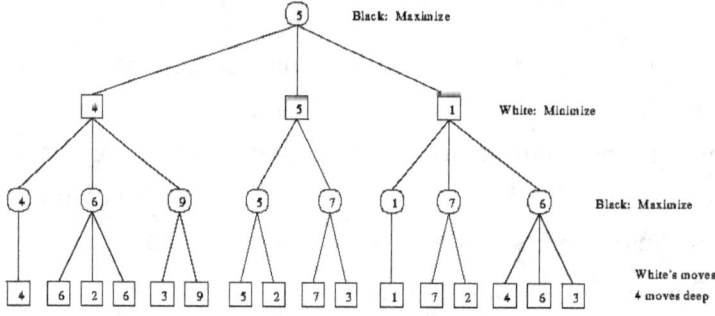

The minimax algorithm: a simple AI for evaluating future outcomes and choosing the best path

In the Great Simulation of life, suppose there is another "function" which is ranking these possible futures, and we at some subconscious level are choosing which of those possible futures and branches we may want to take from the present forward, just like in a video game!

5. Observables and conditional rendering.

When we have a 3d video game, we map out the world using 3d models. In some games, we allow user-generated content that stays in the world even after we log out of the gameplay session so that other players can see it.

In video games, this "model" of the "world" exists outside of the character's perception. In a trick meant for optimization, we don't "render" the whole world on every single player's computer. We only render the part of the world that the player is in, and then usually only for a certain point of view at a certain time. It would be impractical to render the entire world!

Moreover, in 3d video games, there are techniques to optimize the rendering based upon what the player is looking at. These techniques were pioneered in first person shooters like Doom and now used heavily in VR headsets.

A philosophical question that comes up in both Quantum Physics and in Video Games is that if no one is in a particular part of the 3d world—i.e no one is observing it, or no player is there—does the particular possibility exist?

Just like Schroedinger's mysterious cat, which is neither dead nor alive until someone observes it, the world of video games relies on a player being logged in to render the world. If no one is logged into a particular room or a particular world, what state is it in? For example, what happens if there are no players logged into any of the servers of an MMORPG like World of Warcraft? The servers are running but nothing generally happens until a player logs in to observe what is going on, not unlike Quantum Physics.

Spiritual and Mystical Traditions

The next few reasons reflect interesting parallels between some of the spiritual and religious traditions, particularly the Eastern traditions and the Simulation Hypothesis. If you're not into that, skip to reasons #9 and #10.

6. *The World is an Illusion*. In many mystical traditions, particularly in Buddhism and Hinduism, we are told that the world around us is actually an illusion. *Maya*, the Sanskrit word for illusion, is used to describe the world we see, and *Brahman*, is the real world.

In Buddhism, the idea is that to "wake up" you have to recognize that the world around us is an illusion. In fact the term "Buddha" means literally "awake".

In modern terms, they might just be describing a type of video game that we are all caught within, not unlike the HoloDeck from Star Trek. We are caught inside the illusory world, while there is a real world just beyond that we cannot normally perceive unless we "wake up".

In fact, there is a branch of Buddhist Yoga called Dream Yoga, which is used to help us "wake up". In Dream Yoga, a form of lucid dreaming, participants are taught to realize that the dreams we go through at night are "simulated" experiences. By learning to recognize that we are in a simulation, we can "wake ourselves up". The idea is that if we can do this in the "fake" worlds of dreams, so that we can do it in the "fake world" of real life—which is also a simulated reality!

7. *Multiple Lives, Points, Levels & Experience.* According to many eastern traditions, we are actually going through multiple lives, gaining experience in each life and moving up to different levels of "evolution".

In early video games like Pac Man or Space Invaders, each player also had a number of lives—the player accumulated points until the character was killed. The player could "continue" from the place they died, or could "start over" until the dreaded "GAME OVER" flashed on the screen.

In MMORPGs, the player usually has a character which stores up a certain set of experiences between gameplay sessions (the character's state).If we start over, the player of course remembers the skills they have gained in previous lives, but the character starts over with zero values in their state.

This is analogous to how in some Buddhist traditions, when we are born, even though we retain the tendencies of previous lives, we cross the "river of forgetfulness" when we "start over". In these traditions there is still someplace that we store all of our experiences and our points. Where? It's not explicitly stated, but it sure sounds like they are uploaded to some kind of "cloud server".

In some traditions, we go through multiple lives on the wheel of reincarnation. Sure sounds like a Video Game to me!

Let's look at Western religious traditions. As I was growing up in the Islamic tradition, I was told that there was "scorecard" that was being kept for us in this life—every good deed was recorded ("swab") and every bad deed was recorded ("haram") and depending on the score at the end of your life (and on Judgement Day, the day of Kayamath) you would go to either Jannat (Heaven) or Jahannam (Hell). In the Christian traditions, there is also the idea of the two angels on each shoulders and the idea of going to Heaven or Hell (with Purgatory thrown in for good measure). Again, we have the same idea: of a player game-state that is uploaded somewhere "outside" the rendered world.

8. Quests, Karma and God-like AI

In the eastern traditions, our experiences in life are not random; there is a system that is keeping track of what we think and do, and then creating situations in the world to deal with our past actions, called Karma.

Now if you were going to design a seemingly open-ended game, a simulation that can track billions of players, you would need to keep track of quests and achievements for each person.

In today's video games, the quests/achievements/challenges are the same for each player. However, it's not very difficult to envision a more sophisticated video game where quests were chosen based on the past experience of the player. And like in a particular level of a video game, the player could be confronted with similar challenges, again and again, until they are able to pass the challenge.

To accomplish these kinds of "personalized quests" you would need to synchronize across a very large base of "players" and "NPC" or non-player characters (billions of concurrent players in the Great Simulation). You would also need to figure out which group of other players might be compatible, right now, in the moment, in a specific section of the 3d world, to a player's quests. The result of each interaction in the game could have lasting consequences, leading to more challenges in the future.

Some intelligence would need to keep track of billions of concurrent players (something we can't do yet in any video game today). It would seem that an Artificial Intelligence system would be ideal for this kind of task. It may not even need to be that intelligent, as long as the rules were clearly defined and it could scale infinitely!

Let's move from the East to the West, to a more traditional religious framework. In these religions everyone prays to God. Let's assume for a moment that God is real. What is God? What kind of intelligence, if it existed, could keep track of so many, billions of individual prayers and timelines? What could keep track of whether on judgement day, you are to go down to a deeper, less pleasant level ("Hell") of hte game, or go to a higher, more pleasurable level ("Heaven"). You guessed it—an extremely sophisticated AI.

Final Reasons

Moving away from spiritual traditions, let's come back to science for our final two reasons.

9. Player Characters (PC) vs. Non-Player Characters (NPCs)

Nick Bostrom, on the faculty at Oxford University, has long been a proponent of the simulation hypothesis. The argument that he makes is different—that civilizations are unlikely to survive and if they do, then they would have powerful computers that can do "ancestor" simulations. We are more likely, concludes Bostrom, simulated consciousness than actual biological beings. From his famous paper:

One thing that later generations might do with their super-powerful computers is run detailed simulations of their forebears or of people like their forebears. Because their computers would be so powerful, they could run a great many such simulations. Suppose that these simulated people are conscious (as they would be if the simulations were sufficiently fine-grained and if a certain quite widely accepted position in the philosophy of mind is correct). Then it could be the case that the vast majority of minds like ours do not belong to the original race but rather to people simulated by the advanced descendants of an original race. It is then possible to argue that, if this were the case, we would be rational to think that we are likely among the simulated minds rather than among the original biological ones

As a video game designer, this reminds me of our attempts to create realistic "NPC"s or non-player characters. As games have gotten more sophisticated, these AI characters have gotten more sophisticated. We may rapidly be approaching AI which can pass the Turing Test, which is an AI that is indistinguishable from a human being (if you were conversing with them).

I recall early text games like Zork had players that would talk to you and attempts to make these characters realistic. AI has advanced well beyond that but we do not currently have NPCs which can pass the Turing Test. Once we do (in 10 years? In 100 years? In a thousand years), the possibility that people we are interacting with inside a simulation are NPCs goes up considerably. Professor Bostrom thinks that "we" are the simulated consciousness.

10. Speed of Light, Wormholes, etc.

It is curious that in our Universe, as far as we can tell, the fastest that we can travel from point A to point B is the speed of light. This also happens to be the speed of electrical systems and electromagnetic waves. In a normal video game, the fastest we would be able to send information from one player to the next would be over electrical wires. Why would the fastest we can travel through space be the same as the speed of electromagnetic waves, unless our idea of space was being generated by some form of electromagnetic wave?

In the Virtual World of *Second Life*, if you try to go from point A to point B, you would be stuck traveling through the "space" of the game and would have to move slowly—whether you were walking or flying. On the other hand, you could instantly teleport to another part of the game at which point a different part of the 3d world will render around you.

Do we also have this ability in real life? Some physicists have theorized wormholes, or Einstein-Rosen bridges, which would allow us to tear through the fabric of spacetime to shortcut the fabric of space and time. You could think of it as a backdoor—basically a teleport in video game terms.

© Laguna Design/Science Photo Library/Corbis

Wormholes allow us to get outside the 3d world to go from one place to another

Conclusion

These are just some of the reasons why we may be living in a Video Game after all, the Great Simulation. I haven't even gotten into some of the more esoteric or psychological reasons (which would take a whole book unto itself).

As computer science and artificial intelligence rapidly advance their capabilities, it may be possible to create a simulated world that looks and feels as real as our own. Video games, which started out with simple rules about what can be done and simple 2d worlds, have advanced rapidly into a MMORPG (massive multiplayer online role playing games) with millions of players interacting in a simulated world. As computer technology advances, the chances of creating a billion player plus simulated world like our own is rapidly approaching.

Moreover, Quantum Physics gives us a description of the universe (or multiple universes) that doesn't make sense from the perspective of an "objective reality" but requires observation by some consciousness. These sometimes incredible findings defy common sense, unless we are living inside a video game rather than a physical reality and consciousness is the equivalent to us "logging into" the system.

Eastern traditions, particularly Buddhist traditions, have long contended that we are living in world of illusion, and that we go through multiple lives trying to work out our individual quests, all of which are stored beyond the "rendered world". There is a giant system that not only stores this but creates new situations for us to get our "achievements". Sure sounds like a Video Game to me.

All of these areas, Computer Science/Artificial Intelligence, Quantum Physics, and Eastern spiritual traditions point to one likely scenario: That we are living inside a very sophisticated Video Game, which I call *The Great Simulation.*

Like all simulations, our world may only be real while the "simulation" is running.

This reminds me of a quote from the British intellectual, Havelock Ellis, about dreams. He said:"Dreams are real while they last. Can we say any more of life?"

Is this really matters?

What if our universe is something like a computer simulation, or a virtual reality, or a video game? The proposition that the universe is actually a computer simulation was furthered in a big way during the 1970s, when John Conway famously proved that if you take a binary system, and subject that system to only a few rules (in the case of Conway's experiment, four); then that system creates something rather peculiar.

What Conway's rules produced were emergent complexities so sophisticated that they seemed to resemble the behaviors of life itself. He named his demonstration The Game of Life, and it helped lay the foundation for the Simulation Argument, its counterpart the Simulation Hypothesis, and Digital Mechanics. These fields have gone on to create a massive multi-decade long discourse in science, philosophy, and popular culture around the idea that it actually makes logical, mathematical sense that our universe is indeed a computer simulation. To crib a summary from Morpheus, "The Matrix is everywhere". But amongst the murmurs on various forums and reddit threads pertaining to the subject, it isn't uncommon to find a word or two devoted to caution: We, the complex intelligent lifeforms who are supposedly "inside" this simulated universe, would do well to play dumb that we are at all conscious of our circumstance.

The colloquial warning says we must not betray the knowledge that we have become aware of being mere bits in the bit kingdom. To have a tipping point population of players who realize that they are actually in something like a video game would have dire and catastrophic results. Deletion, reformatting, or some kind of biblical flushing of our entire universe (or maybe just our species), would unfold. Leave the Matrix alone! In fact, please pretend it isn't even there.

The basic idea is that the intelligent lifeforms that have evolved inside a simulation are somehow made non-viable, or undesirable as samples, once they become aware of the simulation that they live in. Their own awareness of their plight (their environment) somehow excludes them from being valuable experimental samples. Samples that are aware of the truth of their simulated environment can, or will, compromise themselves, the simulation, or both.

So to avoid this possibly cataclysmic fate, some put forward a kind of survival strategy of "We better not know", and if we do know, "We better play dumb". It's a position that comes with several interesting problems. The first of which should be obvious enough; having just read the last few paragraphs, you are now irrevocably in the know regarding the theory, whether you actually believe the universe to be a simulation or not. Reading this very article is potentially putting reality itself, or maybe just the continuation of our species, at extreme risk. That is supposedly how flimsy the cosmos is to the grandest secret of its truest nature—The universe can be unraveled with the simple transmission and comprehension of just a few sentences describing its features. Only a handful of axioms that explain the environment are apparently enough to destroy us all. Something about this theory feels unlikely, because it means that if you have a deep enough textbook on the nature of reality, the very act of reading it is enough to unmake reality. That sounds a lot like a literary device out of an H.P. Lovecraft short story; imagine an obscure occult science text so dangerous that to utter its very table of contents is enough to return the whole cosmos to total chaos.

Another issue to consider is in the conceivably deeper purposes for simulating a life-sustaining and life-evolving universe. Conceding the problem of anthropomorphizing the motives of our hypothetical simulation-designers, let's nonetheless indulge and imagine ourselves in their position.

If your simulation includes evolving conscious entities that are allowed to develop an intellect (learning), and they have a recursive method to expand and explore that intellect (science), then it is likely that over time and after enough observations those entities will inevitably bump into the "writing on the wall", as it were.

In the case of our own universe, physicist Tom Campbell of NASA has argued that the constant speed of light, the observer effect, and the Big Bang—all matter, energy, and physical laws arriving simultaneously out of nowhere—are tells of just such a situation. Brian Whitworth has published several papers on how the physics we experience could be easily explained with computable analogs. Martin Rees's book Just Six

Numbers could be argued as a whole set of tells. Max Tegmark summarizes the position in the PBS documentary The Great Math Mystery:

"If I were a character in a computer game that was so advanced that I were actually conscious, and I started exploring my video game world it would actually feel to me like it was made of real solid objects made of physical stuff. Yet if I started studying, as the curious physicist that I am, the properties of this stuff, the equations by which things move and the equations that gives the stuff its properties, I would discover eventually that all these properties were mathematical. The mathematical properties that the programmer had actually put into the software that describes everything."

Via Tegmark's thinking we can assume that if the physics and/or nature of any given universe that lends itself to be described through mathematics or exhibits mathematical constants, then it can be surmised to be analogous to, or a derivative of, a computer simulation—even by the entities within that simulation. In other words, if you can compute it, it's likely the result of a computer itself.

In the case of our hypothetical evolving life forms, their science, if it is robust enough, should show that their universe is indeed logically the result of a computer simulation. Otherwise, what is the value of all their science?

We could call this the Simulated Intelligence Hypothesis. If you grow an evolving intelligence in a simulated environment it should, given enough time, be able to deduce, infer, or observe that its environment is indeed the result of a computed simulation. If this is true then it should lead to an interesting circumstance: an evolving intelligence within a simulated environment **cannot** be occluded from the fact that its environment is a simulation, given enough time and a robust enough science. This we could call The Sims Situation—You **cannot** evolve an intelligent sample inside a simulation whilst keeping that simulation hidden indefinitely. Eventually their science will reveal their circumstance, unless of course there is some kind of outside intervention—The same kind of intervention that we should supposedly play dumb in an effort to avoid provoking. Nevertheless, let's return to imagining the evolution of our simulated lifeforms.

If we have a simulated universe that provides a platform for intelligent lifeforms to evolve, we could break these lifeforms up into at least 3 categories: (1) Simple, (2) Complex, (3) Savvy.

1.	Simple, they can make decisions and engage meaningfully with their environment.
2.	Complex, they record history as well as develop sciences, cultures, artifacts, and arts.
3.	Savvy, they are conscious of the fact that they are in a simulated universe.

Once an intelligence moves from a Complex orientation to a Savvy orientation, it has crossed an ontological Rubicon that divides these two distinct viewpoints. We could call this divide the Edge Threshold. If we put any real weight into the computer running this intelligent lifeform evolving universe simulation, then we might in fact hope that it grows something slick enough to figure out what's really going on. Not just for the sake of amusement either, but for an insight into our own motives and nature as simulation-designers. We would actually want a Savvy intelligence inside our simulated universe. The reason why is very simple: If we only have access to observe intelligent lifeforms that are restricted to **not knowing** that they are in a simulation, then our own sample pool and thus knowledge base will always be restricted to intelligences that are out of the loop. Complex level lifeforms (like human beings just prior to the computing revolution) would still be complex and interesting, but they would by definition always already be operating from an ontological ignorance of the true nature of their environment. They would be complex indeed, but far from savvy.

On the other hand Savvy lifeforms would probably be extremely likely to produce fascinating forms of expression, technology, novelty, social organization, and so on. They would also likely begin to create their own life-producing simulated universes themselves. They may even attempt to signal their outside simulation-designing hosts somehow. Therefore I, as part of the original hypothetical simulation-running team, would be extremely hesitant, if not downright protective, of that Savvy sample's survival and evolution—That is if I were to interfere at all. What could possibly give me more insight into what I, the original simulation creator and maintainer, have done than this Savvy sim living in my ever-growing mock universe? Would I really throw out the sim that realized they were in The Sims? Indeed, evolving a sim that realizes they are in The Sims might feel like I'm actually getting my computational weight's worth—That goes especially if I was putting in all this effort to power and evolve a simulated universe in the first place. If our simulated universe is inadvertently an intelligence test for the evolving life forms inside it, then I'd hope we grow a winner. A sample so intelligent that it can actually see the code at the edge of matter is likely a sample we'd benefit from studying. It's not too far removed from teaching great apes to sign.

All of this presents another interesting circumstance to evolving intelligent lifeforms in a simulated universe in the first place. If they, the sims inside, are given enough time to develop their intellects and sciences, then bumping into the truth that they are products of a simulated environment seems nothing less than an inevitability.

In other words when evolving intelligent lifeforms in a simulated environment, either the outside simulation-designers always eventually intervene or the evolving sims inside always eventually figure it all out—barring that they, or their sciences, don't collapse beforehand.

To recap: First, if the Simulation Hypothesis is true, then the Simulated Intelligence Hypothesis is likely also true—an evolving intelligence in a simulation will eventually become aware that they are in a simulation, barring extraordinary intervention.

Second, if the Simulated Intelligence Hypothesis is true than it should lend credence to The Sims Situation—an evolving intelligence in a simulated environment cannot be denied from the knowledge that it is in a simulated environment forever. In other words you **cannot** evolve an intelligence in a simulated environment, and also hide the fact that the environment is a simulation.

Third, this leads us finally to The Savvy Inevitability—if the Simulated Intelligence Hypothesis and the Sims Situation are true, then crossing the Edge Threshold (the ontological divide between Complex and Savvy intelligences) should be assumed as inevitable, given enough time to evolve any given intelligence sample.

Ergo, if all of the above is correct, the hypothetical simulation-designers likely anticipate the eventual emergence of intelligent life forms that can accurately sense what their environment truly is. The simulator(s) may even relish the moment of paradigm shift for their sims in the same manner that adults celebrate their adolescent going off to build their own lives and families.

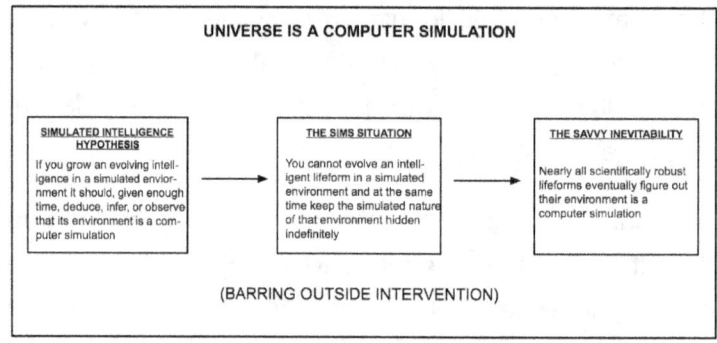

Figure 1 — Evolving intelligent sims

Outside of the assumption that a Savvy sample is valuable in the way just outlined, there are other problems with the previously mentioned "playing dumb" suggestion. The notion that we should (or even could) occlude our "outside" observers, the simulator(s), or ourselves from whatever knowledge we may have about our environment, is not only probably impossible, it is also metaphysically unreasonable. "We better not know", even if it is the correct recourse, is impossible to maintain. Ethically, this notion is odious in that it is not only ultimately anti-science, anti-intellect, and indeed anti-evolution, but it goes on to actually assume punishment for such evolutionary developments, which are in part outside of the evolving intellect's hands. We can't be held responsible for natural discoveries, just as we can't help but see the sun. They are the very fingerprints of the gods, so to speak. We can only truly be made responsible for what we do with natural discoveries; we cannot be made responsible for the fact that we can actually make these natural discoveries. Arguably, nearly all conscious life is defined by its ability to sense its environment. Discovering that the environment is a computer simulation, if that is the case, is a natural consequence of the environment itself.

In summary, if you are evolving intelligent life in a simulated environment, you must expect its simulated nature to be eventually discovered by its inhabitants as a logical consequence of your intelligent lifeforms' evolution.

For these reasons any anxiety regarding our own awareness of evolving within a simulated universe should probably be dismissed outright, because if we are, it would be impossible to hide it from our own, or any other evolving intelligence, indefinitely. If something waits to be discovered and the universe itself provides a platform to develop evolving intelligent lifeforms, then its eventual uncovery is inevitable. As George Berkeley repeated, "To be is to be perceived".

It may very well be a crucial point of existence to discover evidence that this is a simulated universe, if that is the case. The evolution of such a Savvy intelligence is likely far more interesting to the simulator(s), given the Savvy intelligence's likelihood to develop insightful technologies and forms of expression for not just the benefit of the Savvy sample in question, but for the simulator(s) as well. In the possibly endless number of simulated universes, each nested within the other, where in all directions you find simulated universe within simulated universe, like an evolving fractal upon itself, perhaps it is also inevitable that once an intelligence begins to build computers and simulate universes themselves, as we already do in laboratories around the world today, then the questions and ideas that we are wrestling with in this field are likely commonplace throughout the universe, if not the multiverse. Perhaps all this too informs the simulator(s) as well. Perhaps the road that we choose in building our own simulated universes enlightens the creators of the simulated universe that we occupy—Maybe the path we choose informs the path they chose, or didn't choose.

There is a term in professional wrestling called kayfabe. Similar to the suspension of disbelief, it means that wrestlers should always be in character in order to make the overall melodramatic narrative feel exciting and palpable to the fans, even though they too are aware that the entire exchange is scripted beforehand. We all know the blood flowing in a horror film is only dyed corn syrup, nonetheless the false reality is maintained in order to enjoy the spectacle. We are reaching a point in simulism and digital physics where it may be time to drop the kayfabe and peer more deeply into the question: What does it actually mean to be Savvy?

If we are in a computer-simulated universe, we must embrace this new horizon of learning—as we have with heliocentrism, DNA, and evolution before it. We obviously mustn't fear it or pretend that it isn't there. If a rock is truly code, then that is the universe's responsibility, not ours. If the universe is a computed simulation then so too is universal Savviness inevitable for all evolving intelligences that are fortunate enough to survive its slings and arrows. If this is a Matrix then we should probably see what happens when we begin to think and act like it is. Perhaps accepting this is the beginning of kindergarten and the teacher is only moments away from entering the room. Perhaps Morpheus is waiting to give us our phone call.

Is this a Virtual Reality kinda thing?

"It has no relationship whatsoever to anything anchored in some kind of metaphysical superspace. It's just your cultural point of view [...] Travel shows you the relativity of culture."

— Terence McKenna

Human civilization has always been a virtual reality. At the onset of culture, which was propagated through the proto-media of cave painting, the talking drum, music, fetish art making, oral tradition and the like, Homo sapiens began a march into cultural virtual realities, a march that would span the entirety of the human enterprise. We don't often think of cultures as virtual realities, but there is no more apt descriptor for our widely diverse sociological organizations and interpretations than the metaphor of the "virtual reality." Indeed, the virtual reality metaphor encompasses the complete human project.

Virtual Reality researchers, Jim Blascovich and Jeremy Bailenson, write in their book Infinite Reality; "[Cave art] is likely the first animation technology", where it provided an early means of what they refer to as "virtual travel". You are in the cave, but the media in that cave, the dynamic-drawn, fire-illuminated art, represents the plains and animals outside—a completely different environment, one facing entirely the opposite direction, beyond the mouth of the cave. When surrounded by cave art, alive with movement from flickering torches, you are at once inside the cave itself whilst the media experience surrounding you encourages you to indulge in fantasy, and to mentally simulate an entirely different environment. Blascovich and Bailenson suggest that in terms of the evolution of media technology, this was the very first immersive VR. Both the room and helmet-sized VRs used in the present day are but a sophistication of this original form of media VR tech.

Today, philosophers and critics have pointed out that businesses such as McDonald's and Starbucks are like virtual realities in and of themselves. They have a specific and immersive decorum as well as sanctioned behaviors, symbols, and even philosophies. When you enter Starbucks, you enter Starbucks World. In contemporary jargon, these are called hyper realities—they are microcosms with their own purposes and messages. Disneyland and Times Square are the epitome of consumerist hyper realities in the United States. These hyper realities are cloned (copied and pasted) and hold a global footprint in an ever-homogenized worldwide monoculture. They are a touchstone of the global capitalist project; many stores in many locations that are nearly exactly the same. (Similarly, even restaurants that aren't franchise mega-chains offer differing atmospheres; competing little worlds to wine and dine in.) Where did the hyper realities that typify contemporary life get their start? What happened between the cave paintings, and these franchises that nearly everyone on the planet today knows intimately well? I'd like to suggest they got their start with the codification of certain places of worship and the belief systems that joined them.

A simple illustration of the origin of our more complex cultural virtual realities is found in the temple or the church, which acted as the centerpiece of many cultures as they began their voyage into modernity. When we strip the church of the concepts and objects about it, what are we left with? Unoccupied, we are left with a mere building. Yet as we add the corresponding accouterments into and around this building, its virtual reality generating effects amplify and multiply. A church has its altar, its sacred texts, costumes, rituals, sermons, perspectives, symbols, architecture, and so on. All of them are meaningful. The religion is built from this assemblage. Outside, the church is just a building. Inside, the church is a virtual reality—the nodal point of a given religion and a given people. They all work together to reinforce a very specific perception of the world.

Indeed, no one ever actually 'enters a church'. One in fact stumbles headlong into the **idea** of a church—a hyperreal onslaught that the very constitution of the church is purposefully designed to generate. Entering a church is really entering a church-shaped thought. The church building was an early virtual reality headset. From within the church building one looks outward from it and magically the world becomes that religion. The primordial incarnation of this building-sized headset was none other than the very same image-laden, torch-lit caves of our pre-architectural ancestors.

We see this virtual reality-ness in all the objects around and inside a given church or temple, but one very blatant example can be seen in the Christian handiwork of stained glass art. We have here a night on literal representation of key features of contemporary virtual reality technology: filtering and projection. The stained glass is a projective filter that works in both directions simultaneously: light coming into the building is transformed to bring the cultural program of meaningful images into the interiors of the sanctuary where they are contemplated and dogmatized; and back out of the building where the observers inside look outward to a terra firma that is now obfuscated or filtered by the media-messages embedded in the stained glass. The stained glass itself is an evolution of the cave painting. Stained glass would go on to evolve into the pixel. Indeed, stained glass was really a stop between the cave painting and the pixel.

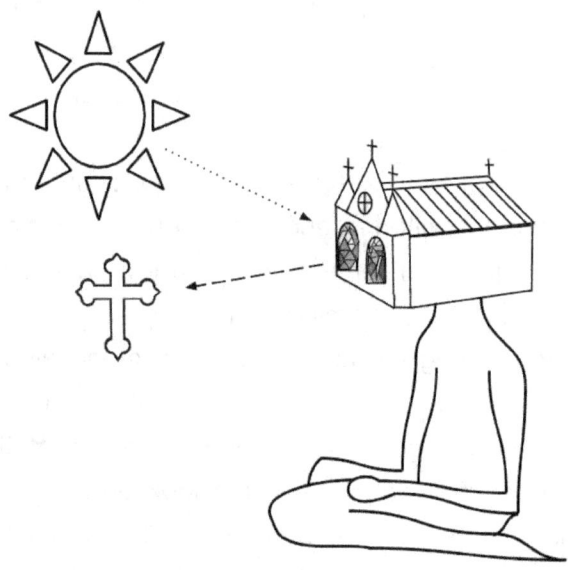

Take another criterion of human civilization and culture in terms of the virtual reality metaphor; language. Regarding text, Kevin Kelly has stated:

"The human mind is actually, has a propensity, a natural gift to move into other realities. When you are reading a book, a novel, when you're totally engrossed in a story, particularly one that's not visual, that you're imagining in your own mind, you're creating a kind of version, a kind of virtual reality."

When we read we decode the text.   That translation directs the theater of our minds to run or play out a given simulation ("See Spot run!   Run Spot run!"). This whole phenomenon of reading and imagining takes place in the invisible holodeck of our minds (more on the term 'holodeck' later). Taking this analogy and bringing it back to the 'inner' virtual reality of the 'voice in our heads', one reads a religious text that is then projected outward, creating a now religious-ized 'external' reality. This is how the vision of a Christian world or a Hindu world is actualized: by deeply absorbing and projecting text-induced mental simulations like "I am the way, the truth, and the life. No one can come to the Father except through me". Once I have faith and believe this to actually be true, I am then living in a Christian virtual reality. I have imagined this particular program into being. I have assimilated x-religion's VR and now live and think in it.

Certainly not all religions can be said to be 'true'. All these different religions are supposedly interpretations of reality or the human condition. The mathematical likelihood of all religions being entirely true is zero, for, despite overlap, they contain different codes, perspectives, accounts, conclusions and so on. They represent humanity's endless struggle with the pressing matter of our shared circumstance; that circumstance being: existing, living, and dying in a vast, mysterious universe. What all these religious interpretations share is that they are not at all dissimilar to virtual realities. They are all self-contained little worlds. However, the virtual reality metaphor doesn't stop at religion. Similarly, different cultures and civilizations are no more 'true' than any other. They too are self-contained little worlds. The virtual reality metaphor includes cultures, ideologies, and all other kinds of frameworks and belief systems. Communism, atheism, scientism, Freudianism are as much cultural virtual realities as the perspectives of the world that come from say totalitarian North Korea, or American fundamentalist Evangelical Christianity. They have different rules, but they are all bubble-like points of view that change what would otherwise be the raw experience of the world into their own code, their own vision of how things are or ought to be.

Take the concept of a nation. A nation is really just a set of notions; their only extra active value is that the notions of a given nation are **mandated**. Laws and legislation, orders, decrees, calendars, cycles, and taboos are each VR nation's programming—their cultural code of conduct. They represent what is permissible and accepted in this world or that. A flag is a VR designating icon, a technology, that whips and colors our minds as much as it does the wind, the sky, and the otherwise uninterrupted terra firma. Our navigational and national lines that crisscross the face of the earth are invisible, imaginary, virtual lines. Where one nation begins and another ends marks the boundaries between separate sets of notions, separate virtual realities. Kings, politicians, lawyers, judges, soldiers, police, executioners, and other "officials" represent an entire class of enforcers of the notions of a nation. These are the rules and rulers of any given cultural VR world. Guns, badges, robes, gavels, jumpsuits, chains and legalese have VR generating effects that make the processes of 'officialdom' appear as if they are legitimate, objective, incorruptible, and deep.

Since, like religions, societies seemingly can't approach a more 'true' society; all that might be said about x-culture versus y-culture in terms of which is 'better' might be argued in terms of how well each nurtures the wellbeing and freedom for all the people, animals, plants, and other environmental factors in each. So other than considering an across the board prosocial and ethical gauge, they are all nonetheless always already entirely self-contained relative virtual worlds—none more 'true' than any another.

The robustness of the virtual reality metaphor spans not just religions, cultures, nations, ideologies, and other belief systems, but actually goes straight down into the individual. The individual perpetuates their own personal virtual reality—their reality tunnel as described by Timothy Leary and Robert Anton Wilson. Wilson states:

"Once you look down at your reality tunnel, whether your reality tunnel is Ohio Methodist or New York Jewish or Morin County hippie or Tokyo capitalist Zen Buddhist or Iranian Muslim fundamentalist, once you get to the level when you're outside of your reality tunnel looking down at it you can compare reality tunnels and then you're at a higher level of intelligence already because you are no longer a conditioned mechanism just following the reality tunnel that was accidentally imprinted or conditioned and you can start choosing between reality tunnels."

Reality tunnel may be a new term for some, but its simplicity in conveying the altogether all too well known immediate experience in the differences between say 'being American' as opposed to be 'being Vietnamese' is unmatched. Even phrases like "to have blinders on" or "tunnel vision" mean the inability to access or appreciate another point of view other than one's own preferred cultural virtual reality, or VR programming. One can't look beyond it. One can't deeply consider other points of view as they are more or less glued into their favorite virtual reality; that being their culture, their belief system, its agenda, its definitions of classes, self, others, and so on. Christians and capitalists alike read their given reinforcing texts, and critique the texts of those they deem outsiders or even enemies. They then spam the world and their peers with the would-be revelations of their world, their reality tunnel. And a reality tunnel is very much what is induced when you strap yourself into a VR headset! As one might imagine, all this talk of reality tunnels puts the focus on the ego.

The ego is the first and final enforcer of a given cultural virtual reality, a given reality tunnel. Part of the process of ego generation and calcification within a certain virtual reality gestates in private experience, with the phenomena of conscious and unconscious self-talk. First, one is both physically and psychically immersed in a given cultural VR. Then our minds chatter away, finding concepts, words, ideas, images, symbols, slogans, behaviors, rituals, billboards, logics, (dis)beliefs, fears, frameworks, memes, heroes, villains, and interpretations—all to either dismiss or indulge within that cultural VR. The ones we're most attracted to we cling onto, even if they are sadomasochistic or result in neuroses and pathologies, cognitive dissonance, unhappiness, violence—it doesn't matter. People are hard pressed to relinquish their reality tunnels and all the easy or favorite answers that they offer. What human beings have proved over the centuries is that they can believe or disbelieve almost anything—reason is frequently moot. This chatter, dismissal, comparison, and indulgence builds up the levels and dimensions of the waking ego. Our thoughts grow our sense of self in this way. Our conscious personality (and often what we 'claim to be' in terms of ideology, religion, philosophy, class, career, and so on) is what living in human-made virtual reality cultures and frameworks ultimately and inevitably creates. We accept our roles, becoming projectors, filters, propagators, true believers, subscription customers, evangelists, defenders, critics, missionaries, 'Romans', and so on. We are active players in our favorite cultural virtual reality super-drama and our playing, our indulging, keeps it all afloat.

In considering what we supposedly are and what we are not, it is interesting to mention that in gender and queer theory we find concepts that sexual identity is just as much a virtual reality as anything else we've been discussing. Gender, in these interpretations, can be as non-fundamental and virtual as any religion is. Judith Butler has explored a key concept here with performativity: gender is intimately tied with the performance of gender, which is irrelevant to biological sex. "Girls will be boys and boys will be girls," as The Kinks aptly observed. Furthermore, the human body is (supposedly) the first filter of the 'external' information that we call 'the world.' If this is true, then the world can only ever reflect our own bodily senses. So even the body itself could be viewed as a virtual reality bubble as well. The body is the first filter taking in the input of the cosmos and all its manifestation. On a physical level the funnel of our bodily organs receiving information from the universe always distorts the universe into the shape of our own senses. This is why we can only physically see a few bands of colored light. We are only directly privy to 0.0035% of the total electromagnetic spectrum. In a human body you can't see the whole spectrum; you can't see all of reality as it truly is. You only have access to a human-centric version of reality. A version that amounts to a simulation of reality provided by the human body and mind. In science and philosophy this has been called naïve realism—human bodily senses are deeply limited in their ability to accurately perceive the world as it truly is. Anaïs Nin said; "We don't see things as they are. We see things as we are."

Finally, there is the entire faculty of thought itself, and with it, imagining. Recall Kevin Kelly's comments on reading at the beginning of this paper: "[When reading a book] you're imagining in your own mind, you're creating a kind of version, a kind of virtual reality." In a similar line of reasoning, Blascovich and Bailenson write:

"'Virtual reality' typically conjures up futuristic images [...] But we believe that virtual reality really begins in the mind and requires no equipment whatsoever. Have you ever spoken face-to-face with someone whose mind wandered off? [...] Hungry people imagine what they'll eat. Overweight people imagine being skinny."

Imagining, and indeed thought itself is the first, most immediate form of virtual reality (alongside bodily sense data). Similarly, the mind has often been referred to in both Eastern and Western literature as working from 'images.' Yet 'images' today implies something static, and thought is anything but static. Our mental images move about chaotically, giving the impression of an animation. Take this analogy one step further and we can easily substitute 'animations' with 'simulations.' Even 'reasoning' is very much the same as simulating. And simulation, or simulating, quickly becomes analogous to virtual reality. In the language of popular culture, thought and the mind is very much like the aforementioned holodeck from Star Trek. Like the holodeck, the mind is like a room that will become anything you or others tell it to become. Almost anything you tell it (program it) to become, the mind will oblige. This can be achieved through words, grunts, language, and text but also through any and all forms of comprehensible media. You, the reader, have been playing out simulations in your own mental holodeck as you've read this paper. This is how we manage to both imagine and participate in such a diverse ecosystem of vastly differing nations, religions, cultures, ideologies, opinions, reality tunnels and so on. Virtual reality is how we've made our human world.

As we have seen, the virtual reality metaphor relates to many domains of human experience; from how our bodies take in information, to how our minds work, to the impact that cultures, nationalities, and religions make on our point of view. This is the utter strength of the metaphor of virtual reality and why it is foundational to some philosophies and religions, though frequently presented using other language (i.e. māyā, skepticism). There is likely no more singularly important consideration than the consideration of alternative worlds, illusory worlds, projected worlds, and manipulable worlds. In the contemporary cinematic jazz mythology of The Matrix, Neo's awakening to the presence of the Matrix is not so much a cyberpunk fantasia as much as it is a commentary on human civilization, culture, and consciousness as a whole. This contemporary allegory retrieves sentiments found in Plato's Cave, Shakespeare's musing that "All the world's a stage", and much of philosophical and spiritual thought throughout the world. Cornel West brings our attention to the dramatic nature of actually taking on whole and fully confronting this paramount philosophical consideration. West states on the Philosopher's Commentary track on The Matrix:

"What's very interesting is the relation between awakening and danger. Once you begin to question you begin to constitute a threat to whatever authority is keeping track of you."

And then:

"Socratic energy has to do with contesting authority, being deeply suspicious of authority, trying to undermine the assumptions and presuppositions upon which authority is predicated. And this process, which is an endless process, it's an incessant process, but it goes step-by-step and stage-by-stage. And at the very beginning now we get the staging of what happens when one initiates a process of awakening in which you render various authorities relative. You begin to contest and call into question those various authorities."

This point of "render[ing] various authorities relative" is going to be more central as we move forward.

Our situation becomes more interesting when we consider the growing popularity of virtual reality headsets like the Oculus Rift. Given the growing availability of VR gaming headsets to consumers, it's natural to begin conjuring with the psychological, sociological, and ontological auxiliary effects that they may end up engendering. After all, they will be changing previous contexts even as they create new contexts. It seems certain that the proliferation of virtual reality entertainment technology will have psychological effects that bleed out far beyond their intended use and into the thoughts of our daily lives, long after we've put our VR gear down. When they do, they might inadvertently start rendering more and more aspects of authority outside them utterly relative and non-fundamental. A VR gaming induced pan-queerification, if you will. Sentiments may rise like: "This game outside is as virtual as that game inside." The VR headset could underscore an awakening to our already well in place, indeed pervasive, projected human virtual realities (our cultures, etc.) as they exist today. Maybe we'll bump into the joke (or conundrum) that when we take off our VR video gaming visor we aren't really re-entering the "real world" at all. We are only ever re-entering the local fantasia, our own personal fantasia, and our responses to the fantasias of others—a place as constructed and limited by human ideas as the one we just left. The ultimate irony becomes that the apex in spectacle entertainment, the immersive VR, may end up being the final panacea against all forms of ideological fundamentalism, extremism, and dogma, be they Western colonialism or North Korean totalitarian necrocracy. That might be wishful thinking indeed but once you can fit a civilization into a VR, then we'll quickly see that civilization is a VR already.

After all, does it not seem predictable that we are going to test-run different worlds in VR games? Naturally some gamers will be so moved by their experiences there that they may even return to waking IRL culture and attempt to mold it in similar ways. Does it not seem inevitable that we will also test out new forms of conditioning, indoctrination, brainwashing, and propaganda using VR? What about when political parties begin having their national events in VR spaces? Can't you see the VR megachurch coming? Do you think that once we're in that VR megachurch we will realize that the churches were all already VRs to begin with? That all that we can declare to be the 'human world' was always just one human-centric VR or another?

The VR metaphor reminds us that all of our institutions are fundamentally projections. We give these projections (and the virtual worlds they create), power by participating, and most importantly, by **indulging** them as legitimate. All cultures and civilizations are relative. So much so, we might well remind ourselves through this VR metaphor if we are to remain steadfast in seeking whatever can be found and developed far beyond their assumed thresholds and limits of vision. Perhaps the cultural apocalypse ('apocalypse' as in 'unveiling') we require in order to free ourselves from the bondage of our current ecocidal project can also be found with this metaphor. Maybe VR will give us the psychic breathing room necessary to re-examine what are *fundamentally* *our* creations—currency for instance. Breathing room for a new vision and a new culture to develop that doesn't so breezily permit catastrophe upon catastrophe. Indeed, culture wouldn't be a problem if our current attempts at culture didn't create so many problems (i.e. externalities and classism).

Ultimately, the speed, variety, liquidity, and accessibility of VR games will begin to challenge the ways of life outside them. After all, if life is different or even better in an entertainment-based game VR, why shouldn't our cultural virtual realities mutate to be equally as pleasant, if not better?

Almost too simple to possibly be true, Jiddu Krishnamurti often repeated; "Thought is responsible for all of this." *Thought **is** responsible for all of this*. It's a comment that demands consideration, especially because we rarely think about what thought is ('simulations'), let alone what it has unleashed upon the world. We have projected this nightmare scenario and followed it through mercilessly and diligently. It did not arrive in a vacuum. We built this place and fostered these conditions. We imagined it and made it, ad infinitum.   Every man-made disaster, intentional or otherwise, is largely thanks to one virtual reality or another. Even industrial accidents that occur under the watch of multibillion-dollar corporations often occur because of a fixed perspective on profit, and a lax perspective on what seems to be almost anything else. We caused these problems, or excused them, or permitted them, thanks to each cultural VR's framework, that being their rules and values.

Maybe VR will remind us that all of this is so. We are living within cultures for sure, but really these cultures are made of thought, and both thought and culture are analogous to virtual reality. They are projected simulated worlds and scenarios. Such a universally relative perspective is really a radical embrace of subjectivity as being an obvious fundamental player in the human enterprise. There is no objectivity in this regard. There is no objectively 'true' civilization, nor a 'true' religion. Any civilization is built and maintained by projected thoughts, associations, actions, images, behaviors, rules, and so on. Admissions such as these frequently generate vertigo. People generally don't like the arguments for near total subjectivity—because they often give off an air that there is, as the saying goes, "Nothing to hang your hat on". Indeed the rendering of major icons of reality and authority as being relative is almost always characterized by an experience of extreme disorientation. This is why Neo vomits at the feet of the revelation that the world he's been living in is a total illusion. (He repeats, "I don't believe it! I don't believe it!") Our ever-diverse human worlds were always ever just our own minds creating virtual realities to play in. Chogyam Trungpa Rinpoche captured it well with the comment; "The bad news is you are falling through the air, nothing to hang on to, no parachute. The good news is there is no ground."

So if all we've made, and all we think, are deeply analogous to VR, the question should come: What is there that is not a VR, or even like a VR? What isn't our human-made VR masquerading as the real? What is fundamental? It may be better to suggest an approach, rather than claim any particular fundamental reality (although, I will do this later anyway). Terence McKenna has suggested one such approach. He advocated; "[A] philosophy not made around the campfire. But philosophy based on the acquisition of extreme experience. That's how you figure out what the world is. Not by bicycling around in the 'burbs but by forcing extreme experience." McKenna's suggested approach is through the well-known cultural vaporizing effects of psychedelic experiences. Peter Sjöstedt-Hughes has given presentations on the historic use of consciousness-altering compounds by philosophers from the Ancient Greeks to Aldous Huxley in the pursuit of knowledge gained from beyond one's culture. He even argues that Plato's Cave is a perfect allegory for the benefits of the psychedelic experience. Pioneers in the computer revolution like Steve Jobs, Douglas Engelbart, Kevin Herbert, as well as the founders of Google are known to have had important encounters with psychedelics. Dr. Kary Banks Mullis won the Nobel Prize for his LSD-fueled DNA research leading to the invention of PCR. Carl Sagan and John C. Lilly were also well-known fans of various psychedelics. Artists of all stripes swear by the value of visionary intoxicants in their role of inspiring some of the most beloved masterpieces of all time. In other words, literature suggests that there is a deep value in the compounds, plants, substances, and practices that help us human beings "break on through to the other side"—That "other side" being the domain beyond our familiar and pervasive human VRs and frameworks.

It is interesting to note that VR headsets and visors actually mirror the psychedelic experience in many ways. They mirror it in that when you don the headset you enter a new world. You put on the new head. And when you do, you see another possible vision of how reality could be. When you are done and take off the headset, you are hit with a second insight: the relativity of this world, this cultural virtual reality, or universe, to the headset-VR world you just exited. Returning from your trip is as valuable as going on the trip in the first place, because now you have a more robust mechanism by which to compare worlds. Suddenly they are both non-fundamental. Suddenly they are relative. If you've never left Sri Lanka or the Amish way of life for example, then that's your threshold of knowledge and the height of your interpretive powers. What we are left with after these encounters with cultural relativity (regardless of the means by which it is achieved) is that, to quote McKenna; "Most of reality is illusory. It's just we do each other the courtesy of not pointing this out." However it should be deeply appreciated that the VR headset experience at this time cannot rival the awesome panoply of titanic revelation that digesting certain plants and compounds can offer. VR offers a parallel to psychedelics (some, McKenna included, have argued that VR is the technological shadow of the psychedelic experience), but it is not at all the psychedelic experience proper in all its quaking, annihilating, and mind-expanding glory.

Beyond doing whatever you can to temporarily escape your local VR programming, an admission would be that **consciousness itself is fundamental to all our virtual realities.** Consciousness is the media through which all our cultures, religions, civilizations, thoughts, and reality tunnels play out. So although what we have created can be regarded as virtual realities, consciousness itself doesn't necessary fit that criterion. Consciousness is real, 'Canada' and 'Canadian' is imaginary, is virtual. Consciousness plays within the framework of 'Canada' and 'Canadian' but it isn't those constructs on a fundamental level. Consciousness is not virtual reality, though it uses virtual realities to operate in. What are we without our virtual realities? We are alive and indeed life itself. We are the end result of billions of years of cosmological evolution. And we are consciousness. One of the all-time best comments for underscoring the insidious depth of this virtual reality projecting faculty of the mind is found in a koan popularized by non-dualist author Adyashanti: "At the end of the day a real Buddhist realizes that there is no such thing as a real Buddhist." So it is not as Morpheus says; "As long as the Matrix exists the human race will never be free." We will always be building a Matrix to see, move, and operate through. Instead it is that as long as the Matrix exists and remains **deeply unacknowledged as a Matrix and ever-indulged as "true"** the human race will never be free. Consequently, nor will the global ecosystem likely survive; for as long as it remains a mere supporting character—or worse, has no role whatsoever—in our reality tunnels, the prominence it deserves in our decisions cannot be realized.

Let us not be like innocent, forgiving, or unassuming children in the face of our entirely relative, projected, cultural virtual realities. For they more or less entirely dominate our lives and thoughts. Nonconformity is frequently met with alienation at the very least. At this point our virtual realities also make up a likely cause of death for the planetary ecosystem. The capitalist VR is one such obvious culprit in terms of large-scale environmental and species devastation. At one point in the past these forms of engagement seemed to have risen up organically alongside the evolution of our meaning-making neocortex. Today however it would be naïve to assume that they are harmless—especially considering the expansion and proliferation of various forms of power centralization, and the violence that typifies them. Our cultural virtual realities have values and institutions that clearly exist to keep the power status quo well maintained and far removed from the majority. They also devastate every corner of the planet that is within reach, frequently in the pursuit of transforming it into altogether virtual "profit". McKenna pointed out:

"Someone rather intelligent once said, 'Language was invented so that people could lie.' In other words it gives you that fudge factor of obfuscation where someone says you know, 'Why did you do that?' Well the best approach is, 'I didn't do that!' You know, 'You thought I did that. What you thought you saw you didn't see!' In other words I suppose that lawyers are probably the people who have done the finest work with language and behind them politicians. And the true potential for language to elevate and unite the community was early on betrayed into the production of illusory and ideological goods which could then be marketed among the people and to spread confusion."

This is as unsentimental, unflattering, and indeed honest as it gets. The leaders, profiteers, true believers, indeed the leading-edge of the lie, are more than likely in on the con—for they execute undying efforts, regardless of how absurd or atrocious, to keep it all maintained.

So, what's the valuable or worthwhile course of action considering all we've covered? Wilson suggested; "On a planet that increasingly resembles one huge Maximum Security prison, the only intelligent choice is to plan a jailbreak."

The only way out of any cultural VR is to first accept that you are more than likely always already on the user-end of one or another. The first thing a fish must do if it is to escape the water is to identify that it is in fact in water. That there exists both water and, not water. After making that discovery, it can then begin the slow climb of exploring the hitherto before unknown environments and dimensions, as well as the accompanying new states of being necessary to participate in them—that's legs, lungs, wings, and the like. Step one is seeing your culture for the virtual reality that it is. This is the essence of "awakening" as the colloquialism goes. It is also the essence of becoming "hip". Simple enough: If you were born in another country and grew up in another culture, another VR, you'd like have a different opinion on a myriad of subjects. But, like the fish before it discovered the land, it is difficult if not impossible to imagine prior to experience.

Culture is a virtual reality with which we see and move through the world—and cultures are entirely of our own making. As we have seen, these VRs exist in myriad domains and forms of human experience and behavior. Why is it so important to realize everything we've gone over is a virtual reality? So that you, dear reader, feel empowered to change it, to overcome it, to not accept it as "business as usual" or "the way things are." These are all virtual realities. None of them are anchored to any transcendental wisdom or truth. How these VRs have informed us isn't fundamentally true. Largely, they are arbitrary. They amount to convenient contrivances. Our game is just a game. The rules are our own. There is no need to indulge any culture or framework as being the final word on reality or social organization. Indeed, **we** are the elephant in the room. When we discover that we are all responsible for the shadows dancing on the wall, we will realize that we are both the cause and the solution to all of our problems. From here new frontiers shall open. For, it is the goal of any system of intelligence to transcend itself. This is paramount in assessing the world we have created and the world we are leaving behind not just for our future ancestors, but for all lifeforms on this planet. Ralph Waldo Emerson is credited with the remark; "The end of the human race will be that it will eventually die of civilization." If we bear in mind pollution, warfare, national or cultural tensions, and the unbridled excesses of capitalism, then Emerson's comment on civilization is far from obscure. Similarly, McKenna stressed; "It makes no sense whatsoever to speak of a human future. There is no human future. It's inconceivable, given where we are today, that to speak of the human world a thousand years from now or five hundred years from now, it is literally, it either doesn't exist, or it's beyond our power of imagining." Our world today has a few perilous demands: drop the old games (our projective filters and made-up rules), see through them, outgrow them entirely if necessary, and begin to imagine and participate in better ones. As Mark Booth closed his seminal and endlessly peculiar book The Secret History of the World, "Imagination is the key".

Just imagine virtual realities that are more meaningful, beautiful, ecumenical, compassionate, sustainable, efficient, and indeed more loving to play. In a word: wiser. The call upon the present generations is to radically shift gears and awaken to what we are really doing. We will accept our responsibility for this crisis or we will go down in the history of the universe as another menagerie of pseudo-intelligent space bumpkins at the far end of the galactic arm who collapsed into dust under the weight of their own illusions. This is the warning shot echoing through modernity fired by none other than Mary Shelley in Frankenstein; or, The Modern Prometheus. We will end at the hands of none other than both our own psychic and physical creations—our virtual reality worlds—unless we evolve them.

Rendering these cultural VRs relative is an essential part of the process in transcending and evolving them. Again, why do they demand to be transcended and transformed? Because they simply aren't up to snuff; they do not match the moral and ethical reasoning that is necessary to handle the pan-destructive forces that our fathers and grandfathers have already unleashed upon the surface of the earth.

It's really that simple.

Our most powerful and influential cultures are far from benign. Culture eats nature; our worst VRs eat the world.

The challenge and the gift that we have given ourselves is a whole planet on the brink—the ultimate narrative, the life or death game par excellence. The creator's creation now threatens the continuity of life itself, when its hope was always to uplift. All in all, it's a very exciting time to be alive. You won't get a better opening act to the primate's next stage of awakening than the one where it has fallen into its own otherwise brilliant, multi-millennia in the making trap. The question bubbling up as the Information Age gives birth to the Virtual one is; "What will end up being born out of our totally humanized enclosure when we push hard enough against the thresholds of our collective fantasy worlds?" You will know where you truly are by the writing on the wall, coupled with the acidity index of the ocean.

Breaking the core

Silicon Valley, tech culture, and most nerds the world over are familiar with the real world version of the question are we living in a Matrix? The paper that's likely most frequently cited is Nick Bostrom's _Are you living in a Computer Simulation?_ Whether or not everyone agrees about certain simulation ideas, everyone does seem to have an opinion about them.

Recently, the Internet heated up over Elon Musk's comments at a Vox event on hot tub musings of the simulation hypothesis. Even Bank of America published an analysis of the simulation hypothesis, and, according to Tad Friend in an October 10, 2016 article published in New Yorker, "two tech billionaires have gone so far as to secretly engage scientists to work on breaking us out of the simulation."

It is this notion of "*escape*," of breaking out of our simulation, that has inspired me to write this article.

Where are we really?

Like everything truly intelligent, the simulation hypothesis demands we have a deep appreciation of paradox—an appreciation that is frequently lacking in simulism dialogs. That paradox is simply this: if this universe is a simulation, that means, quite paradoxically, it is here, but it is also not here. We are here and we are also not here. As Einstein reportedly pressed upon other physicists when they struggled with the information rendering-like nature of wave-particle duality, along with other spooky quantum observations, "Do you really believe the moon isn't there when you're not looking?" The authentic simulist answer must patently be, "There is no moon." This is the inevitable and disturbing thread that simulation theory researchers and philosophers largely fail or refuse to grok, but its logic is sound and obvious.

When you play an MMORPG are any of those objects "*real*" or "*there*"? No—They are information. Is that level or map in the MMORPG real? Can your avatars escape it? No, because neither the levels nor the avatars are really there. Mario is not really in the Mushroom Kingdom. It's all just numbers in a computer. It is digital information. The game universe only **seems** to be there—but it isn't, and we aren't.

Now back to us—why does our physics ruleset permit entanglement, or retrocausality, or wave-particle duality, or quantum erasure, or teleportation, or tunneling? Because all that, along with spacetime, mass, gravity, light, and spin simply isn't really real in a physical or deterministic sense. It's not really there in the way we normally assume. They are all just effects in the virtual reality, and experiments have shown that the effects are rendered as needed. Brian Whitworth said it well in his paper Simulating Space and Time:

VR theory is only on the table because objective reality theory doesn't explain modern physics. In an objective reality time does not dilate, space doesn't bend, objects don't teleport and universes don't pop into existence from nowhere. We would not doubt the world's objective reality if only it behaved so physically, but it does not. Adjectives like "*strange*", "*spooky*" and "*weird*" apply, and common sense concepts like object, location, existence, time and space simply don't work. The world of modern physics doesn't behave at all as an objective reality should.

So the "escape" begins first and foremost with appreciating the paradox of it all that means thinking about it, being with it, seeing it:

The Universe is here and it is not here

You are here and you are not here

You aren't even really in a room

There is no moon

It's just information

It's just data

You cannot really be "in" a video game, because being in a video game really means you are a trick of information that only **appears** to look like a whole you and a whole universe—**but it isn't really**. So how can you escape something you are not really in? How do you escape something you **only appear** to be in? This is the central issue.

It is appropriate to say that this paradox marks one of the most essential ideas in all simulation, virtual reality, and digital mechanical scenarios. This is where we have to begin any discussion of the simulation hypothesis, or its sister models, or the idea of "escape." We have to appreciate the paradox involved wholly before going anywhere at all. We are here and we are also not here. It is a waste of time and resources to move forward without having this paradox at the forefront of our attention.

Furthermore, it is a waste to assume that some physical machine (one that's in our simulation) is going to be developed that can rip a hole in spacetime (in the video game), and that will somehow lead us to the "true" universe.

Technology will not help you

Although, I admit ignorance regarding what approach these rumored billionaire-encouraged researchers are taking, I will throw in my two cents anyway and claim that making a machine won't work. At this point there are still too many assumptions in play to rely on technology to provide the key:

1) A machine in a video game can somehow get avatars out of their video game universe.

To me, hard high tech leading to an escape is an unlikely avenue. You are more likely to break out of a maximum-security prison with a dry-erase marker than you are to develop some kind of hardware within a simulated universe that can somehow get you out of it. The reason why is because relying on a machine is still thinking from within the logic of the physics of the video game itself (its spacetime, gravity, geometry, spin, etc.) You very well might be able to perform experiments to detect whether or not the universe is one kind of simulation or another, but that's a far cry from technology breaking us out of our universe.

2) More video game won't automatically generate to keep you inside your video game universe; or, your machine will mysteriously keep breaking down.

Even if you did make such a machine, I anticipate the System behind our simulated universe would simply generate a new, higher wall for you to climb. Or your machine will mysteriously and consistently malfunction and fail ("gremlins").

3) That such a machine won't lead you to some other video game reality and not "*base reality*."

If you did make such a machine, how could you tell the difference between whether or not it was giving you access to "base reality" and not just some other simulated universe? How do you know that the hole you tear in spacetime isn't leading you to some other video game world or another? As Morpheus asks, "*How would you know the difference between the dream world and the real world?*"

So, if the hardware angle is out (which it really should be) is all hope lost? No. The fact of the matter is this kind of thinking is looking in the exact opposite direction. We should be looking more at consciousness and consciousness states than we should the domain of spacetime, geometry, matter, and technology. If the universe is a computer simulation then we should look at the player, not the level. This turn of focus from physical reality to the viewer of reality is exactly the same realization that the founders of Quantum Mechanics wrestled with helplessly in the early 20th Century. Indeed, the "*Observer*" and "*Measurement*" debates continue to this day.

It's all in your head—and you have no head

Consciousness science and research is largely a nascent field. This is due in part to the many assumptions that surround consciousness and the brain as well as there being a general failure of agreement in defining consciousness. The grand poopah assumptions are consciousness is a byproduct of the brain; consciousness will eventually fall in line with material reductionism (consciousness is matter); extraordinary or unusual states of consciousness are negligible brain wetware misfiring; any and all psi effects (telepathy, precognitive dreams, out-of-body experiences, etc.) are all lies, misadventures, quirks, or flukes; first came matter, then came mind.

However, if the simulation hypothesis, or any number of simulism positions are true, then it follows that the brain is virtual information in a video game—just like everything else. The brain that we all assume to be carrying around in our bodies is just our avatar's body's virtual "brain." It's not really real. What about brain damage or damage to the body? Well there are rules to the video game—If you lose a chunk of brain, your data-stream is modified to reflect that. If you lose an arm, your data-stream is modified to reflect that too.

Again, in the simulation models, our whole experience of the universe is a virtual reality—so nothing at all is going on as it seems. There is no moon—it is only *there* when a player requests the data ("looks"). Down on the farm though, it seems like an "observer" "collapses" the "wave." Rather than reality being solid, deterministic, and "out there" it is instead a statistical probability distribution—potential information. This potential information is only ever "rendered" ("collapsed") when a consciousness ("observer") makes a measurement. Game effects only pop up when the player requires them.

So none of it is really real—although it may be safer to say that it is also, paradoxically, *real enough*.

Now the simulism camp I find most interesting (and there are several) was developed by NASA physicist and consciousness researcher Thomas Campbell. He feels that the "*out-of-body experience*" as well as the mystical, religious, extraordinary, and paranormal phenomena that human beings have seemingly stumbled into since the beginning of recorded history is in fact a kind of "breaking out" of our video game ruleset. We simply interpret it as being episodes like "She had an out-of-body experience" due to our bone-marrow assumptions that spacetime and the body are fundamental, when in fact the universe is the result of a computer simulation and everything is information.

Campbell also breaks from Nick Bostrom's now classic thought experiment of our universe being the result of an ancestor simulation created by future posthumans. Rather, Campbell answers Edward Fredkin who argued in Finite Nature and A New Cosmogony (a decade before Bostrom) that basically since a simulated universe can't compute itself, it must be computed in Other. Fredkin states:

As to where the Ultimate Computer is, we can give an equally precise answer; it is not in the universe -- it is in another place. If space and time and matter and energy are all a consequence of the informational process running on the Ultimate Computer then everything in our universe is represented by that informational process.

The place where the computer is, the one that runs that process, we choose to call 'Other'.

In Campbell's model, Fredkin's Other is **Consciousness itself**. Campbell's definition of consciousness is an unusually straightforward one. Consciousness, to Campbell, is any system that contains the following features:

1. Information input (experience)

2. Information recall (memory)

3. Information processing (sense-making; pattern recognition, etc.)

4. Self-modifying feedback loop (learning)

Any system possessing these features, in Campbell's model, can rightly be called conscious.

Campbell's Consciousness is both the consciousness we find manifest in lifeforms and also the very computer behind our universe—Fredkin's Other. It is this outline of consciousness that, when pressed upon by what Campbell calls the "Fundamental Process" of evolution, any number of interactions, lifeforms, universes, realities, or rulesets could naturally emerge. Anything from cellular automata, to a multiverse, to nature's "inordinate fondness of beetles" could subsequently appear. All realities, lifeforms, and interactions are possible under Campbell's two assumptions: Consciousness exists (as defined), and Evolution exists.

From this model, there is no need for a master programmer or an ancestor simulation. Instead, those overlords are chucked outright for a single, arguably dim at first, conscious computer that is always forced to either evolve or die. In the illusory worlds of virtual reality, consciousness itself is entirely real and actually holds center stage.

To Campbell, Consciousness is fundamental. We, our individual consciousnesses, are partitioned parts of The Big Conscious Computer that crunches out this and every other universe and lifeform. So, where we really are is in Fredkin's Other; Fredkin's Other is Campbell's Consciousness. Our avatar—our body—appears to be "*in*" a simulated universe, a video game. While our actual awareness experiences this universe as physical spacetime, both the universe and ourselves are actually an information data-stream processing and occurring in Other.

If Fredkin's Other is Campbell's Consciousness, then almost everything about life, consciousness, the universe itself, and the simulation hypothesis falls entirely into place. This would explain why quantum mechanical observations by and large for almost a century seem to be sensitive to, what physicists have called, "observers", or "measurement." It is because consciousness is the fundamental—indeed the essential—medium through which the simulation must be rendered. Without a consciousness (a player) there is no video game to render and really no need to.

Again, there is no need to simulate or process anything at all without what John Archibald Wheeler rightly called *"observer-participants"*—players. No player, no game.

So, in an interesting twist, the computer behind our simulated universe is our own consciousness; *"base reality"* is Consciousness itself. This is why the future of simulism is in fact consciousness research and exploration.

Getting in to get out

Human consciousness is particularly sensitive to psychedelic experiences. Psychedelic science is a famously taboo arena, largely because of government intervention as well as the sometimes utterly alien and titanic experiences they produce. Yet, in terms of our topic of *"breaking out of the Matrix"* it would be folly to overlook them due to something as anti scientific as stigma.

Anecdotally (and sadly, due to psychedelics' banishment to basement chemistry in the mid 20th Century, the majority of psychedelic research remains anecdotal, as well as historical)—powerful compounds like DMT, ibogaine, and even psilocybin and LSD at high doses are known to produce effects and environments that impact on the users a feeling of being exposed to geometric, mathematical, fractal, and other phenomena reminiscent of a cosmically complex computation. On countless occasions I have been pressed by individuals to elaborate on my ideas about virtual reality and the simulation hypothesis only to later find out that their own psychedelic experiences left them feeling like they had seen into the holy guts and heart of reality, and that it resembled some kind of hyper-intelligent computer system to them.

Peter Sjöstedt-H, a PhD candidate at the University of Exeter, has presented a "*history of the notable western philosophers who took psychedelic chemicals and how this may have influenced their thought—how psychedelics influenced philosophy.*" Sjöstedt-H's psychedelic list includes some of the heavy weights of the standard Western cannon: Schopenhauer, Nietzsche, Bergson, Sartre, Foucault, and more. He writes:

Psychedelic experience has then influenced different philosophers in different ways. Its multifaceted, anomalous, alien, awe-inspiring, and at times terrifying nature is not easily analysed. In fact, it often transgresses the phenomenological criteria by which analysis can take place. But then such novel phenomena can be taken as an augmentation of the phenomenological toolkit rather than as a mere mysterious anomaly to treat with philosophic disregard.

When people say, "*Escape the Matrix*," what they really mean is perceiving and even operating beyond the ruleset of our simulation. Maybe shamans, mystics, meditators, philosophers, and the psychonauts of today have been doing this forever. William Blake put it aptly, "*If the doors of perception were cleansed every thing would appear to man as it is ...*" Furthermore, Professor David Nutt said, "*If you want to understand consciousness, you've got to study psychedelics.*"

A monument to our computational overlords

It has been my own thinking that if we're in a computer simulation, and assuming that simulation is being monitored, then it might be a very interesting turn of events indeed if we decided to build a monument commemorating our realization of this. This monument would act as a signal to our monitors. *"We suspect you are there. We suspect you can see this. We suspect we are in a simulation."* This monument could look like the monolith from *2001: A Space Odyssey*, except it would be black and white, representing binary systems. Or, a large statue of Laurence Fishburne as Morpheus would probably get the point across. What would happen? I don't know—maybe nothing. I don't think a laser beam will shoot out from space and land at its feet to spell out the words *"Hi there! A Winner is You!"* But, I do imagine something strange and far out enough in the margins might indeed occur, although it will likely still be tenuous enough for the dogmatists to reject. Crop circles perhaps—(Needless to say, simulation frameworks in general explain all psi and paranormal phenomena quite elegantly. It should go without saying that if you believe your video game world is really real and something utterly peculiar happens to go down, you might very well be inclined to interpret it as paranormal or supernatural, when in reality it is just the game getting weird on you.)

Nevertheless, I imagine a monument to be a far more effective pursuit than some kind of other hardware or technology springing us loose. I this universe is a computer simulation and some *"they"* are monitoring it from the "*outside,*" they will likely be intelligent enough to get our drift with such a monument. In fact, maybe something like a monument is just what they're waiting for. After all, we've only been addressing each other in the simulism dialog—never the rumored, assumed "them" monitoring it.

Ever play The Sims? If you have then you know that none of your Sims can do anything in secret. We, the player, have total oversight. Here we are discussing breaking out of our video game universe. Do you think "*They*"—if there truly is a "*They*"—don't already know that we're thinking and talking about planning a bust?

What to do?

Why is it all here? Why are we in a simulated virtual reality video game universe anyway? According to Campbell it is to evolve consciousness. Since The Big Conscious Computer is under pressure to evolve or die it has further evolved universe simulations and partitioned itself into seemingly discreet conscious lifeforms, all with the universal goal of staving off high entropy via interacting, learning, growing, propagating, adapting, and so on. To Campbell, our universe is not necessarily the result of posthumans per se, but from an AI that grew universes to interact in so that it could better survive the fundamental process of evolve or die. Here, both life and virtual reality universes end up springing from the same source. Since static states are unstable, the credo seems to have become *go big or go home*.

All you need to get the ball rolling is consciousness (as defined) and an evolutionary impulse of change or die.

But even if Campbell is incorrect, as we consider all the possible paths of inquiry that the various simulism models afford, is it not obvious that the nature and foundation of consciousness, its role in the simulation, as well as the issues of "where" is the cpu behind the universe—and subsequently our location "in" it—must eventually all take center stage? Where is Mario if he isn't really in the Mushroom Kingdom?

Fredkin, said it clearly enough, "If we assume that Finite Nature is true, we discover that surprising progress can be made in looking beyond our own world."

So what is a solid way to begin looking beyond our world? How do you break out of a universe that you only appear to be in? All you Neos out there, if you want to break out of the Matrix, look into the wildly queer and otherwise forbidden domain of consciousness research, psi, the paranormal, out-of-body experience, dreams, meditation, and psychedelics. Indeed, these are the otherworldly themselves—so start with them. This might not be the answer you wanted (some of you being residents of Big Machine Country) but I'll bet you bits to bandwidth that consciousness is the key missing from the simulation hypothesis—and consciousness states, the door. Maybe all that assumed irrationality coming out of shamanism, magic, mysticism, and the Grateful Dead might end up in fact being how to competently exploit Other's operating system.

Do you really ever escape this simulated universe? Campbell argues that you can vividly experience information from other realities, but that all of them are simulated. Furthermore, he argues that getting out of all simulated universes is like trying to get out of consciousness—and can you *really* get out of consciousness? All in all, to Campbell's thinking, *we don't really want to get out of the Matrix. What we want to do is* **get into Consciousness.**

Maybe all we really need to do is close our eyes and pay very careful attention.

174

Experimenting   Simulation
Hypothesis

(A simple explanation of this article is available in next article! You can skip to that if you don't wanna get into details)

Wheeler advocated that "Quantum Physics requires a new view of reality" integrating physics with digital (quanta) information. Two such views emerge from the presupposition that reality could be computed. The first one, which includes Digital Physics and the cellular automaton interpretation of Quantum Mechanics , proposes that the universe is the computer. The second one, which includes the simulation hypothesis suggests that the observable reality is entirely virtual and the system performing the simulation (the computer) is distinct from its simulation (the universe). In this, we investigate the possibility of experimentally testing the second view and base our analysis on the assumption that the system performing the simulation has limited computational resources. Such a system would therefore use computational complexity as a minimization/selection principle for algorithm design.

On the emergence of probabilistic computation. It is well understood in Information Based Complexity (IBC) that low complexity computation requires computation with partial/incomplete information. As suggested in and shown in the identification of near optimal complexity algorithms requires playing repeated adversarial (minimax) games against the missing information. As in Game and Decision Theory , optimal strategies for such games are randomized strategies . Therefore Bayesian computation emerges naturally in the presence of incomplete information. for a history of the correspondence between Bayesian/statistical inference, numerical analysis and algorithm design). Given these observations the fact that quantum mechanics can naturally be interpreted as Bayesian analysis with complex numbers suggests its natural interpretation as an optimal form of computation in presence of incomplete information (it is interesting to note that in the Bayesian formulation of Quantum Mechanics is also logically derived in a game theoretic setting). Summarizing these observations, in the simulation hypothesis, to achieve near optimal computational complexity by computing with partial information and limited resources, the system performing the simulation would have to play dice.

On the compatibility of the simulation hypothesis with Bell's no go theorem. Bell's no-go theorem shows that the predictions of quantum mechanics cannot be recovered/interpreted, in terms of classical probability through the introduction of local random variables. Here, the "vital assumption" [5, p. 2] made by Bell is the absence of action at distance (i.e. as emphasized in [5, eq. 1], the independence of the outcome of an experiment performed on one particle, from the setting of the experiment performed on another particle). Therefore Bell's no-go theorem does not prevent a (classical) probabilistic interpretation of quantum mechanics using a "spooky action at distance" .Here, the simulation hypothesis offers a very simple explanation for the violation of the principle of locality implied by Bell's no-go theorem , the EPR paradox , Bell's inequalities violation experiments and quantum entanglement: notions of locality and distance defined within the simulation do not constrain the action space of the system performing the simulation (i.e. from the perspective of the system performing the simulation, changing the values of variables of spins/particles separated by 1 meter or 1 light year has the same complexity).

On rendering reality It is now well understood in the emerging science of Uncertainty Quantification that low complexity computation must be performed with hierarchies of multi-fidelity models. It is also now well understood, in the domain of game development, that low computational complexity requires rendering/displaying content only when observed by a player. Recent games, such as No-Man's Sky and Boundless, have shown that vast open universes (potentially including "over 18 quintillion planets with their own sets of flora and fauna") by creating content, only at the moment the corresponding information becomes available for observation by a player, through randomized generation techniques (such as procedural generation). Therefore, to minimize computational complexity in the simulation hypothesis, the system performing the simulation would render reality only at the moment the corresponding information becomes available for observation by a conscious observer (a player), and the resolution/granularity of the rendering would be adjusted to the level of perception of the observer. More precisely, using such techniques, the complexity of simulation would not be constrained by the apparent size of the universe or an underlying pre-determined mesh/grid size but by the number of players and the resolution of the information made available for observation.

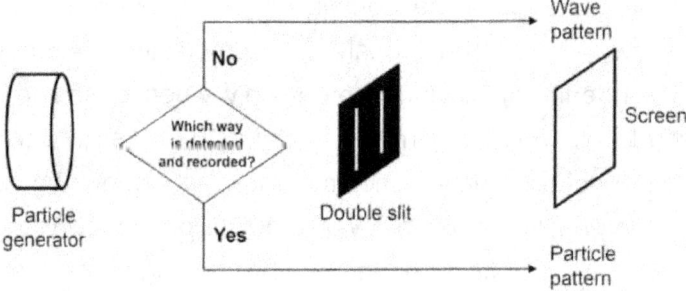

Figure 1: The classical double slit experiment [14, 2] with which way detected before or at the slits. We write "wave pattern" for interference pattern, and "particle pattern" for non-interference pattern.

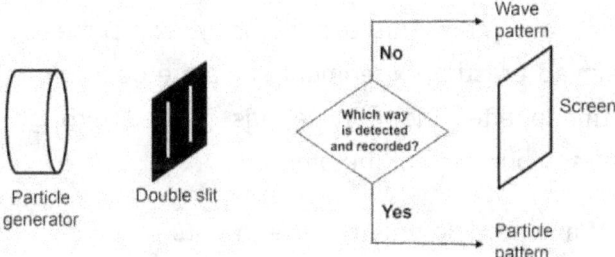

Figure 2: The delayed choice experiment. The choice of whether or not to detect and record which way data is delayed until after each particle has passed through a slit but before it reaches the screen.

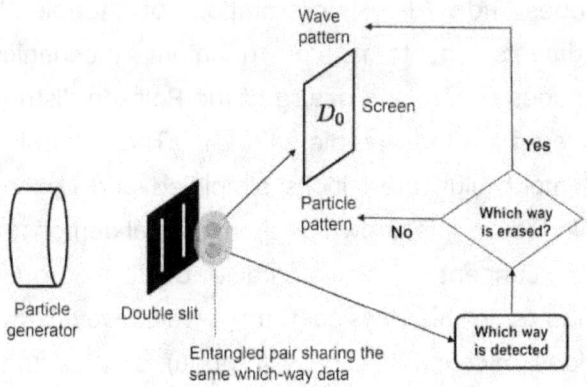

Figure 3: The delayed choice quantum eraser experiment. Which way data is collected before, at, or

after each particle has passed through a slit, however, this which way data may be erased before the particle hits the screen. This experiment is sometimes called a delayed erasure experiment since the decision to erase is made after the particle has passed through a slit (chosen one path or the other).

2. Wave-particle duality experiments

Although the double slit experiment has been known as a classic thought experiment since the beginning of quantum mechanics, and although this experiment was performed with "feeble light" in 1909 and electron beams in 1961, the first experiment with single photons was not conducted prior to 1985 (we refer to, which also describes how the interpretation of "feeble light" experiments in terms of quantum mechanics is ambiguous due to the nature of the Poisson distribution associated with "feeble light"). The double slit experiment, illustrated in its simplified and conceptual form in Figure 1, is known as the classical demonstration of the concept of wave/particle duality of quantum mechanics. In this classical form, if which way (i.e. which slit does each particle pass through) is "detected and recorded" (at the slits), then particles (e.g. photons or electrons) behave like particles and a non-diffraction pattern is observed on the screen. However, if which way is not "detected and recorded," then particles behave like waves and an interference pattern is observed on the screen. Since in the classical set up, the which way detection is done at the slits, one may wonder whether the detection apparatus itself, could have induced the particle behavior, through a perturbation caused by its interaction with the photon/electron going through those slits. Motivated by this question, Wheeler argued, using a thought experiment (illustrated in its simplified and conceptual form in Figure 2), that the choice to perform the which way detection could be delayed and done after the double-slits. We refer to for the experimental realization of Wheeler's delayed-choice gedanken experiment. Comparing Figure 2 with Figure 1, it appears that whether the which way data is detected and recorded before, at, or after the slits makes no difference at the result screen. In other words, the result at the screen appears to not be determined by when or how that which way data is detected but by having the recorded which way data before a particle impacts that screen.

Following Wheeler, Scully and Drühl proposed and analyzed an experiment (see Figure 3), realized in, where the which way detection is always performed "after the beam has been split by appropriate optics" but before it is possibly erased (with probability 1/2 using a beam-splitter). We also refer to for a set-up with significant separation in space between the different elements of the experiment. Comparing Figure 3 with Figure 2, it appears that whether the which way data is or is not erased determines the screen result. Again, the result at the screen seems to be determined, not by the detection process itself but by the availability of the which way data. Erasing the which way data appears to be equivalent to having never detected it.

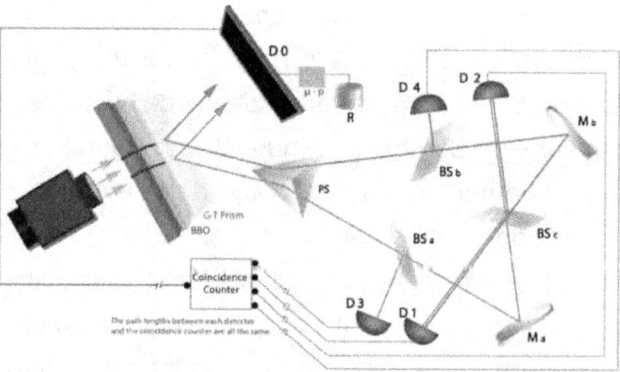

Figure 4: The delayed choice quantum eraser experiment set up as described in .The microprocessor (μ-p) represents an addition to the original experiment and will be discussed in Section 3 and in the Appendix

Remark 1. A remarkable feature of the delayed choice quantum eraser experiment (see figures 3 and 4) is the creation of an entangled photon pair (using a type-II phase matching nonlinear optical crystal BBO: $\beta - BaB_2O_4$) sharing the same which way data and the same creation time. One photon is used to trigger the coincidence counter (its impact location screen D_0 is also recorded) and the second one is used to detect the which way data and possibly erase it (by recording its impact on detectors D_1, D_2, D_3 and D_4). The coincidence counter is used to identify each pair of entangled photon by tagging each impact on the result screen D_0 and each event on the detectors D_1, D_2, D_3 and D_4 with a time label. Using the coincidence counter to sort/subset the impact locations (data) collected on the result screen D_0, by the name (D_1, D_2, D_3 or D_4) of the detector activated by the entangled photon, one obtains the following patterns:

D1: Interference pattern (which way is erased).

D2: Interference pattern (which way is erased).

D3: Particle pattern (which way is known, these photons are generated at Slit 1).

D4: Particle pattern (which way is known, these photons generated at Slit 2).

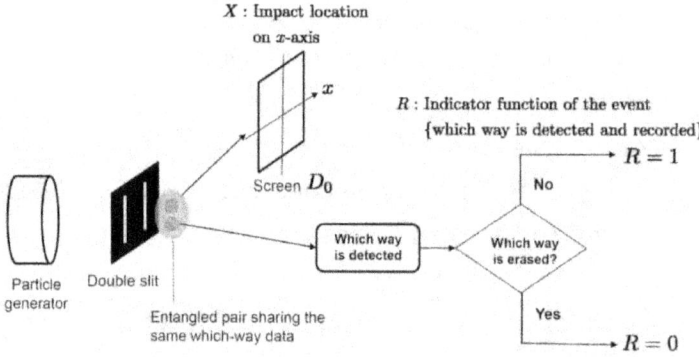

Figure 5: Delayed Erasure Experiment. Which way data is randomly recorded with probability 1/2.

3. Predicting erasure in the delayed choice quantum eraser experiment

We will now describe wave-particle duality experiments aimed at testing the simulation hypothesis by testing the hypothesis that reality is not rendered (or the wave function is not collapsed) at the moment of detection by an apparatus that would be part of the simulation, but rather at the moment when the corresponding information becomes available for observation by an experimenter. More precisely our hypothesis is that wave or particle duality patterns are not determined at the moment of detection but by the existence and availability of the which way data when the pattern is observed. The first test is based on a modification of the delayed choice quantum eraser experiment. In this modification, we use the facts that (1) the entangled pair of photons discussed

in Remark 1 share the same which way data (2) the experiment can be arranged so that the first photon hits the screen (sending a pulse toward the coincidence counter) before the second one reaches the beam-splitter causing the erasure or recording of the which way data with probability 1/2 (but the time interval between these two events must be significantly smaller than the time interval between creation of photon pairs to preserve the information provided by the coincidence counter). The location X of the impact (on the x-axis) of the first photon on the screen (see Figure 5) is then recorded and used to predict whether the which way information will be erased (R = 0) or kept/recorded (R = 1). More precisely by applying Bayes' rule we obtain that

$\mathbb{P}[R = 1 | x \leq X \leq x + \delta x] = \frac{\mathbb{P}[R=1]}{\mathbb{P}[x \leq X \leq x+\delta x]} \mathbb{P}[x \leq X \leq x + \delta x | R = 1]$. Using $\mathbb{P}[x \leq X \leq x + \delta x] = \mathbb{P}[x \leq X \leq x + \delta x | R = 0]\mathbb{P}[R = 0] + \mathbb{P}[x \leq X \leq x + \delta x | R = 1]\mathbb{P}[R = 1]$ and $\mathbb{P}[R = 0] = \frac{1}{2}$ we deduce that

$$\mathbb{P}[R = 1 | x \leq X \leq x + \delta x] = \frac{1}{1 + f(x)} \text{ with } f(x) = \frac{\mathbb{P}[x \leq X \leq x + \delta x | R = 0]}{\mathbb{P}[x \leq X \leq x + \delta x | R = 1]}. \quad (1)$$

Let d be the distance between the two slits and L the distance between the slits and the screen (where X is recorded). Write λ the wavelength of the photons and $a := \frac{\lambda L}{d}$. Using the standard approximations $\mathbb{P}[x \leq X \leq x + \delta x | R = 1] \approx 2I_0 \, \delta x$ and $\mathbb{P}[x \leq X \leq x + \delta x | R = 0] \approx 4I_0 \cos^2(\pi \frac{x}{a}) \delta x$ (valid for $x \ll L$) we obtain that

$$\mathbb{P}[R = 1 | x \leq X \leq x + \delta x] \approx \frac{1}{1 + 2\cos^2(\pi \frac{x}{a})}. \quad (2)$$

Therefore if the proposed experiment is successful, then the distribution of the random variable R would be biased by that of X and this bias could be used by a microprocessor whose output would predict the value of the random variable R (prior to its realization) upon observation of the value of X. This bias is such that, if the value of X corresponds to a dark fringe of the interference pattern and a high intensity part of the particle pattern, i.e. if $\cos(\pi$ xa $) = 0$ and x/a $= 0$, then the photon must be reflected at BS a and BS b (i.e. R = 1) with a probability close to one. Observe that the value of R is determined by whether the photon is reflected rather than transmitted the beam splitters BS a and BS b (which are large masses of materials that could be at large distance from the screen D_0). Therefore, if the proposed experiment is successful, then for values of X corresponding to a dark fringe of the interference pattern, it would appear as if the measuring, recording, and observing of impact location X determines whether the which way data will or will not be erased. Such a result would solve the causal flow of time issue in delayed erasure experiments: detection at D_0 would now determine (or introduce a bias in) the choice, i.e. reflection or transmission, at BS_a and BS_b. However, a new issue would be created: The detection at D_0 deterministically selecting (or, for a general value of X, strongly biasing the probability of) the choice at BS_a and BS_b (reflection or transmission) when that choice is supposed to be random (or, for a general value of X, independent from X). Although this could be seen as a paradox such a result would have a very simple explanation in a "simulated universe": the values of X and R are realized at the moment the recorded data becomes available to the observer (experimenter).

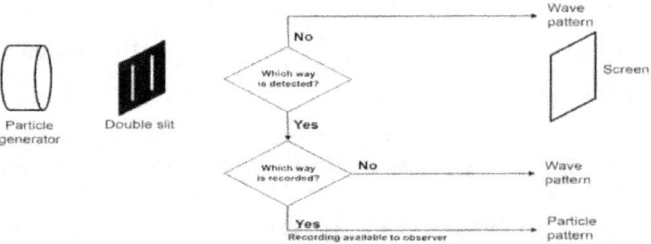

Figure 6: Detecting but not recording "which way"

4 Detecting but not making the data available to an observer

We will now describe experiments, which if proven successful, would provide even stronger evidence in favor of the simulation hypothesis. The following experiments are designed based on the hypothesis that the availability of which way data to an observer is the key element that determines the pattern found on the result screen: the simulated content (the virtual reality) is computed and available to be rendered to an experimenter only at the moment that information becomes available for observation by an experimenter and not at the moment of detection by an apparatus.

In the second experiment, illustrated in a simplified and conceptual form in Figure 6, the which way data is detected but not recorded (which translates into the non availability of the which way data to the experimenter/observer). There are many possible setups for this experiment. A simple instantiation would be to place (turned on) detectors at the slits and turn off any device recording the information sent from these detectors (or this could be simply done by unplugging cables transmitting impulses from the detectors to the recording device, the main idea for this experiment is to test the impact of "detecting but not making the data available to an observer").

This test could also be implemented with entangled pairs using the delayed choice quantum eraser experiment (see Figure 4) by:

• Simply removing the coincidence counter from the experimental setup and recording (only) the output of D 0 (result screen). D 0 should display the wave pattern if the experiment is successful.

• Or by turning off the coincidence counter channels D 3 and D 4 (and/or the detectors). If the experiment is successful, then D 0 should (without the available information for sorting/subsetting between D 3 and D 4) display an interference pattern (and sorting the impacts at D 0 by D 1 or D 2 should also show interference patterns).

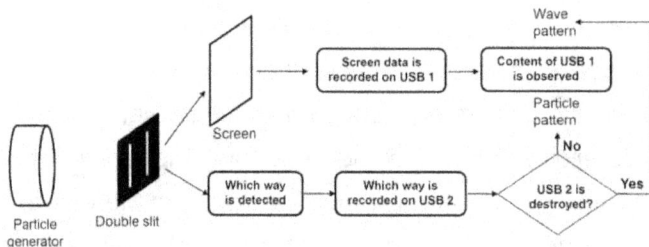

Figure 7: Erasing the which way data on a macroscopic scale

5 Erasing the which way data on a macroscopic scale

In the third experiment, illustrated in a simplified and conceptual form in Figure 7, the decision to erase the which way data is delayed to a macroscopic time-scale. This can be implemented by using the classical double slit experiment shown in Figure 1 where the recordings of the which way data and the screen data (impact pattern) are collected on two separate USB flash drives. By repeating this process n times one obtains n pairs of USB flash drives (n is an arbitrary non-zero integer). For each pair, the which way USB flash drive is destroyed with probability $p_d = 1/2$. Destruction must be such that the data is not recoverable and no trace of the data is left on the computer that held and transferred the data. For n even, one can replace the coin flipping randomization by that of randomly selecting a subset composed of half of the pairs of USB flash drives containing which way data for destruction (with uniform probability over such subsets). The test is successful if the USB flash drives storing impact patterns show an interference pattern only when the corresponding which way data USB flash drive has been destroyed. This test can also be performed by using the delayed choice quantum eraser experiment or its modified version illustrated in Figure 5. For this implementation, one USB flash drive is used to record the data generated by the photons for which X is measured (output of D_0) and other USB flash drives to record the data generated by D_1, D_2, D_3 and D_4 along with the associated output of the coincidence counter.

6 Discontinuities in rendering reality

What determines the result at the screen D_0 (the value of X)? What causes and determines the collapse of the wave function? Or in Virtual Reality (VR) terminology, what causes the virtual reality engine to compute and make information defining the VR available to an experimenter within the VR?

Is it

(I) entirely determined by the experimental/detection set-up?

(II) or does the observer play a critical role in the outcome?

Under the simulation hypothesis, these questions can be analyzed based on the idea that a good/effective VR would operate based on two, possibly conflicting, requirements:

(1) preserving the consistency of the VR (2) avoiding detection (from the players that they are in a VR). However, the resolution of such a conflict would be limited by computational resources, bounds on computational complexity, the granularity of the VR being rendered and logical constraints on how inconsistencies can be resolved. Occasionally, conflicts that were unresolvable would lead to VR indicators and discontinuities (such as the wave/particle duality).

Although the experiments of Figures 5, 6 and 7 have been aimed at testing the simulation hypothesis by testing the moment of rendering, it also possible to design thought experiments where the conflicting requirement of logical consistency preservation and detection avoidance would lead to strong discontinuities.

We refer the reader to the appendix for one such experiment (a hypothetical thought experiment) where the VRs rendering engine would be forced to create discontinuities in its rendering or be constrained to produce a clear and measurable signature event within our reality that would be an unambiguous indicator that our reality must be simulated.

As a secondary purpose, the thought experiment discussed in the appendix will also be used clarify the notion of availability of which way data in a VR.

Acknowledgments: We thank Lorena Buitrago for her help with Figure 4.

The simple explanation of experimental proots

In terms of the major models in physics and cosmology, the simulation hypothesis, digital mechanics, and computation-based interpretations have endured and indeed grown in popularity over the last few decades, making them major contenders to the scientific dialogue. Why simulation and computation make for such powerful analogies is that they offer a useful framework for approaching the paradoxes found throughout quantum mechanics. If quantum phenomena behave frequently as if spacetime is totally moot, that would make sense if our universe is something like a probability-based simulation, a computer, a virtual reality, or a video game. VR would account for the time-tested problems of entanglement, erasure, delayed-choice, particle-wave duality, retrocausality, and all the other queer observations in quantum studies that Einstein announced were far too "spooky" for him to swallow. Nevertheless, quantum mechanics remains the most mathematically precise framework of how natural phenomena act.

Some have argued that this trendy computational-simulation angle is untestable, non-falsifiable, and thus, ultimately irrelevant. A useless novelty of our computer-plagued era. Well no more...

Can the hypothesis that reality is a simulation be tested? We investigate this question based on the assumption that if the system performing the simulation is finite (i.e. has limited resources), then to achieve low computational complexity, such a system would, as in a video game, render content (reality) only at the moment that information becomes available for observation by a player and not at the moment of detection by a machine (that would be part of the simulation and whose detection would also be part of the internal computation performed by the Virtual Reality server before rendering content to the player).

Proposals for doable, realistic experiments for testing the boundaries of our would-be virtual reality universe is itself an achievement. The ease at which such experiments could be carried out is what makes Campbell and company's paper so exciting. None of the experiments Campbell offers are particularly difficult or expensive to implement. They specify, "More precisely our hypothesis is that wave or particle duality patterns are not determined at the moment of detection but by the existence and availability of the which way data when the pattern is observed." The paper offers a set of 6 entirely new quantum experiments that would clearly validate this new perspective.

The focus of this new paper is on the longtime debate of whether or not conscious observation plays a fundamental role (possibly an exclusive one) in collapsing the wave-function, or if environments and apparatuses collapse the wave-function as well:

What causes and determines the collapse of the wave function? Or in Virtual Reality (VR) terminology, what causes the virtual reality engine to compute and make information defining the VR available to an experimenter within the VR?

Is it

(I) entirely determined by the experimental/detection set-up?

(II) or does the observer play a critical role in the outcome?

Under the simulation hypothesis, these questions can be analyzed based on the idea that a good/effective VR would operate based on two, possibly conflicting, requirements: (1) preserving the consistency of the VR (2) avoiding detection (from the players that they are in a VR). However, the resolution of such a conflict would be limited by computational resources, bounds on computational complexity, the granularity of the VR being rendered and logical constraints on how inconsistencies can be resolved. Occasionally, conflicts that were unresolvable would lead to VR indicators and discontinuities (such as the wave/particle duality).

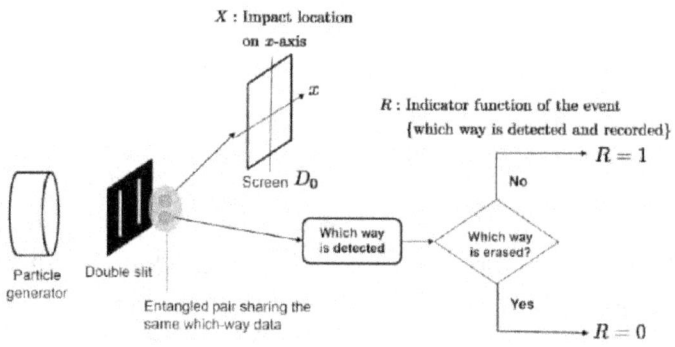

In 2015, the nearly century-long hot debate of whether or not conscious measurement collapses the wave function (https://plato.stanford.edu/entries/qm-collapse/#ProbTail WaveFunc) became positively smoldering with the execution of a delayed-choice thought-experiment originally proposed by John Archibald Wheeler, and carried out at The Australian National University (http://www.nature.com/nphys/journal/v11/n7/full/nphys33 43.html). Associate Professor Andrew Truscott from the ANU Research School of Physics and Engineering said flatly, "It proves that measurement is everything (https://www.sciencedaily.com/releases/2015/05/1505271 03110.htm). At the quantum level, reality does not exist if you are not looking at it." Things do not really exist as we tend to imagine them to exist; they only seem to appear to exist—and they appear to exist only in the presence of an observer. Similar to the experiment performed at ANU, Campbell and company's "first test is based on a modification of the delayed choice quantum eraser."

If Campbell and company's experiments prove that "the observer plays a critical role in the outcome," as the ANU work has, then several important readings fall out from there. One being that Wheeler's intuition was correct; the language of "observer-participants" is in fact a spot-on reading of the role of conscious measurement in relation to a quantum system. Wheeler—a heavyweight in 20th century physics—brought the world everything from black holes, to quantum foam, to an information theoretic reading of physics, widely known by his slogan It from Bit (http://cqi.inf.usi.ch/qic/wheeler.pdf).

Conceptually speaking, an observer-participant is only a stone's throw from the mechanics of a player-avatar in a video game.

Although deeply counter-intuitive to the assumptions of determinism, materialism, and realism—what we are taught in high school science classes—the best way to comprehend how it could be that the universe only exists when you look at it can be found in how players and avatars interact within video game maps. The avatar only seems to move through the level—but it is an illusion. The game's spacetime effects are ultimately just demonstrations that are provided for the player-avatar by a computer. When you play a video game, every level and detail is loaded and rendered only as needed. That's how you can have phenomena that do indeed appear to occur within a spacetime universe, and paradoxically, also have that spacetime behave like it can be both real and moot at different scales. Campbell and company are banking on a similar outcome in their experiments. They write:

It is also now well understood, in the domain of game development, that low computational complexity requires rendering/displaying content only when observed by a player. Recent games, such as No-Man's Sky and Boundless, have shown that vast open universes (potentially including "over 18 quintillion planets with their own sets of flora and fauna") by creating content, only at the moment the corresponding information becomes available for observation by a player, through randomized generation techniques (such as procedural generation). Therefore to minimize computational complexity in the simulation hypothesis, the system performing the simulation would render reality only at the moment the corresponding information becomes available for observation by a conscious observer (a player), and the resolution/granularity of the rendering would be adjusted to the level of perception of the observer. More precisely, using such techniques, the complexity of simulation would not be constrained by the apparent size of the universe or an underlying pre-determined mesh/grid size but by the number of players and the resolution of the information made available for observation.

Nick Bostrom articulated the idea elegantly in his now famous paper Are you Living in a Computer Simulation? (http://www.simulation-argument.com/simulation.html):

Simulating the entire universe down to the quantum level is obviously infeasible, unless radically new physics is discovered. But in order to get a realistic simulation of human experience, much less is needed – only whatever is required to ensure that the simulated humans, interacting in normal human ways with their simulated environment, don't notice any irregularities. The microscopic structure of the inside of the Earth can be safely omitted. Distant astronomical objects can have highly compressed representations: verisimilitude need extend to the narrow band of properties that we can observe from our planet or solar system spacecraft. On the surface of Earth, macroscopic objects in inhabited areas may need to be continuously simulated, but microscopic phenomena could likely be filled in ad hoc.

What you see through an electron microscope needs to look unsuspicious, but you usually have no way of confirming its coherence with unobserved parts of the microscopic world. Exceptions arise when we deliberately design systems to harness unobserved microscopic phenomena that operate in accordance with known principles to get results that we are able to independently verify.

And, in a truly sci-fi twist, Bostrom adds:

Moreover, a posthuman simulator would have enough computing power to keep track of the detailed belief-states in all human brains at all times. Therefore, when it saw that a human was about to make an observation of the microscopic world, it could fill in sufficient detail in the simulation in the appropriate domain on an as-needed basis. Should any error occur, the director could easily edit the states of any brains that have become aware of an anomaly before it spoils the simulation. Alternatively, the director could skip back a few seconds and rerun the simulation in a way that avoids the problem.

The universe is assumed to be a massive size and a massive amount of information. How is it that the universe could be so vast, or appear to be so vast? What could possibly support or cause such complexity, diversity, and life? Well in some ways it has already been done in video games. If this universe is a computer simulation, it makes sense that only what an observer-participant requests is all that needs to exist at any given moment. This would save computing cycles for whatever computational meta-system that supports our simulated universe. It also makes sense as to why all the matter, energy, and the many laws and constants of physics (some of them tuned to mind-bogglingly fine precision) would appear all at one, at the same time, from apparently no where, for apparently no reason—The simulation went GO on day.

At the end of his life Einstein concluded, "Space does not have an independent existence." That means the stuff of the world isn't as objective and independent as it looks. We are not like little cameras looking at a solid world out there at all. In fact, it only appears objective and solid after you've looked. Maybe, its very existence is dependent upon being looked at. When we don't look it exists only as a probabilistic, statistical potential—an unrendered possibility. So without conscious players there would be no game and without the game there would be no players. They are one and the same—wholly dependent upon each other to exist. Hence Einstein's tricky comment above.

Einstein also said, "It is clear that the space of physics is not in the last analysis anything given in nature or independent of human thought. It is a function of our conceptual scheme." Campbell summarized this sentiment from Einstein, saying, "Space is a function of mind."

David Bohm, another big man of science and Einstein's colleague said:

"To meet the challenge before us, our notions of cosmology and the general nature of reality must have room in them to permit a consist account of consciousness. Visa versa our notions of consciousness must have room in them to understand what it means for its content to be 'reality as a whole.' The two sets of notions together should then be such as to allow for an understanding as to how consciousness and reality are related."

These odd, almost wooey statements about consciousness and observation are far from unusual when reading the essays and letters of some of the most influential minds behind cosmology and quantum mechanics. Nobel Prize Winner Eugene Wigner said, "It will remain remarkable in whatever way our future concepts may develop that the very study of the external world led to the scientific conclusion that the content of the consciousness is the ultimate universal reality."

Similarly, Andrei Linde, who accurately predicted the discovery gravitational waves, and one of the heavyweights behind inflationary theories, stated in a 2002 Discover Magazine (http://discovermagazine.com/2002/jun/featuniverse) piece:

"The universe and the observer exist as a pair [...] You can say that the universe is there only when there is an observer who can say, Yes, I see the universe there. These small words — it looks like it was here— for practical purposes it may not matter much, but for me as a human being, I do not know any sense in which I could claim that the universe is here in the absence of observers. We are together, the universe and us. The moment you say that the universe exists without any observers, I cannot make any sense out of that. I cannot imagine a consistent theory of everything that ignores consciousness. A recording device cannot play the role of an observer, because who will read what is written on this recording device? In order for us to see that something happens, and say to one another that something happens, you need to have a universe, you need to have a recording device, and you need to have

us. It's not enough for the information to be stored somewhere, completely inaccessible to anybody. It's necessary for somebody to look at it. You need an observer who looks at the universe. In the absence of observers, our universe is dead."

How to wrap your head around all of this? Philosopher Terence McKenna had an excellent summary of the reading of conscious-observer based wave collapse idea; "Mind is necessary for the universe to undergo the formality of exiting." If observers do indeed render reality, then much of our entire Western physics, philosophy, and metaphysics paradigm is totally shattered. That is why many scientists during the time of Einstein, faced with the same strange experimental results that we are still wrestling with today, made comments along the lines of those above. Max Plank, the godfather of quantum mechanics, said, "We must assume behind this force the existence of a conscious and intelligent Mind. This Mind is the matrix of all matter." And, *"n the last analysis, we ourselves are part of nature and therefore part of the mystery that we are trying to solve."*

But what if the mind Plank refers to is not a perfect deity per se, but rather an imperfect, yet evolving conscious computer?   One that's crunching out VR universes, physics, and conscious players.

If Campbell turns out to be correct and we are in a computer simulation, then there is indeed an answer to Einstein's famous assertion, "Do you really believe the moon isn't there when you aren't looking?"

The answer is emphatically, "There is no moon."

Quantum Phenomena: A computer
analogy

I. The Appearance of Waves

A. Waves with no medium, *as though they were
mathematical formula only*

In our everyday experience, waves are formed by motion
within a medium. Waves come in different varieties.
Ocean waves and sound waves roll outward from a

source through the medium of water and air. A violin string waves back and forth along its length, held in place at the two ends of the medium, which is the violin string. A jerk on a loose rope will send a wave rolling along its length.

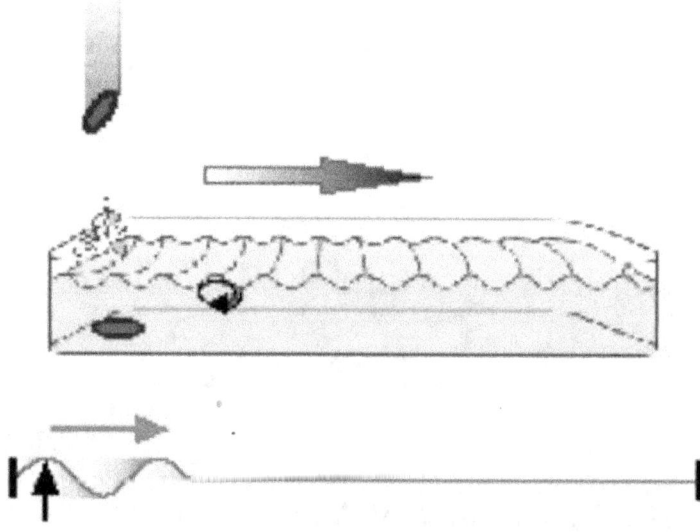

In 1802, Thomas Young demonstrated fairly convincingly that light had the properties of a wave. He did this by shining light through two slits, and noting that an interference pattern formed on a projection screen. Interference patterns are one of the signature characteristics of waves: two wave crests meeting will double in size; two troughs meeting will double in depth; a crest and a trough meeting will cancel each other out to flatness. As wave ripples cross, they create a recognizable pattern, exactly matching the pattern on Young's projection screen.

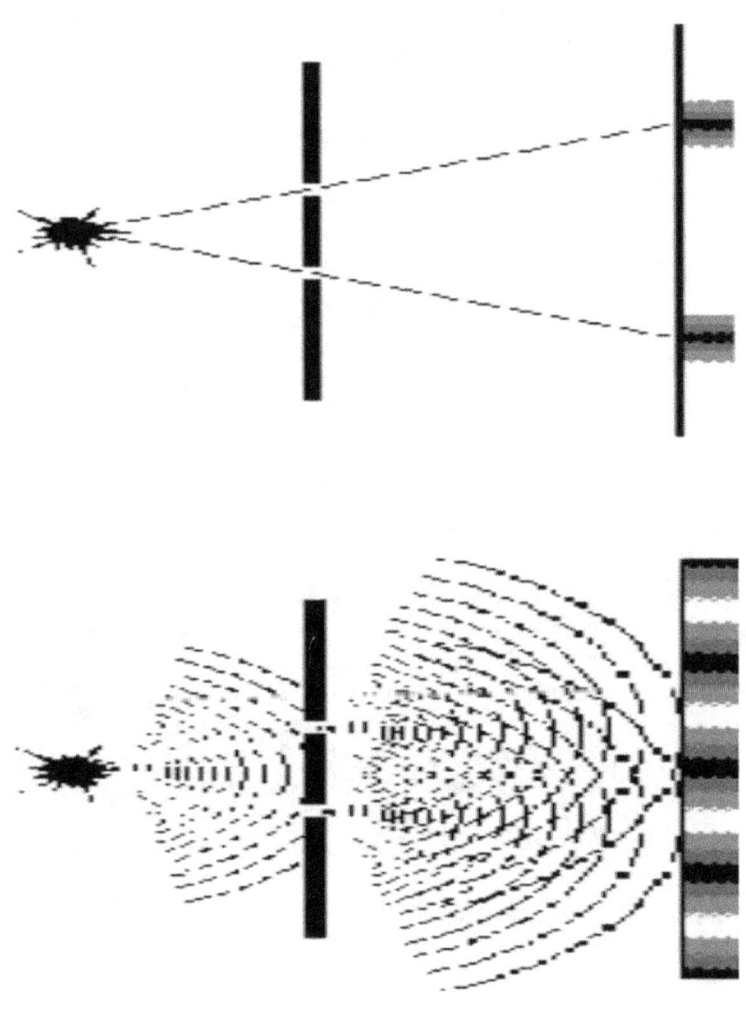

For most of the 19th century, physicists were convinced by Young's experiment that light was a wave. By implication, physicists were convinced that light must be traveling through some medium. The medium was dubbed "luminiferous ether," or just ether. Nobody knew exactly what it was, but the ether had to be there for the unshakably logical reason that without some medium, there could be no wave.

In 1887, Albert Michelson and E.W. Morley demonstrated fairly convincingly that there is no ether. This seemed to imply that there is no medium through which a light "wave" travels, and so there is no medium that can even form a light "wave." If this is true, how can we see evidence of waves at all? Ordinary waves of whatever sort require a medium in order to exist. The Michelson-Morley experiment should have had the effect of draining the bathtub: what kind of waves can you get with an empty bathtub? Yet the light waves still seemed to show up in the Young double slit experiment

In 1905, Albert Einstein showed that the mathematics of light, and its observed constancy of speed, allowed one to make all necessary calculations without ever referring to any medium. He therefore did away with the ether as a concept in physics because it had no mathematical significance. He did not, however, explain how a wave can exist without a medium. From that point on, physicists simply put the question on the far back burner. As Michio Kaku puts it, "over the decades we [physicists] have simply gotten used to the idea that light can travel through a vacuum even if there is nothing to wave."

The matter was further complicated in the 1920s when it was shown that objects -- everything from electrons to the chair on which you sit -- exhibit exactly the same wave properties as light, and suffer from exactly the same lack of any medium.

The First Computer Analogy. One way to resolve this seeming paradox of waves without medium is to note that there remains another kind of wave altogether. A wave with which we are all familiar, yet which exists without any medium in the ordinary sense. This is the computer-generated wave. Let us examine a computer-generated sound wave.

Imagine the following set up. A musician in a recording studio plays a synthesizer, controlled by a keyboard. It is a digital synthesizer which uses an algorithm (programming) to create nothing more than a series of numbers representing what a sampling of points along the desired sound wave *would look like* if it were played by a "real" instrument. The synthesizer's output is routed to a computer and stored as a series of numbers. The numbers are burned into a disk as a series of pits that can be read by a laser -- in other words, a CD recording.

The CD is shipped to a store. You buy the CD, bring it home, and put it in your home entertainment system, and press the play button. The "music" has traveled from the recording studio to your living room. Through what medium did the music wave travel? To a degree, you might say that it traveled as electricity through the wires from the keyboard to the computer. But you might just as well say it traveled by truck along the highway to the store. In fact, this "sound wave" never existed as anything more than a digital representation of a hypothetical sound wave which itself never existed. It is, first and last, a string of numbers. Therefore, although it will produce wave-like effects when placed in your stereo, this wave never needed any medium other than the computer memory to spread itself all over the music loving world. As you can tell from your CD collection, computers are very good at generating, storing, and regenerating waves in this fashion.

By analogizing to the operations of a computer, we can do away with all of the conceptual difficulties that have plagued physicists as they try to describe how a light wave -- or a matter wave -- can travel or even exist in the absence of any medium.

B. Waves of calculation, not otherwise manifest, as though they really were differential equations

The more one examines the waves of quantum mechanics, the less they resemble waves in a medium. In the 1920s, Ernst Schrodinger set out a formula which could "describe" the wave-like behavior of all quantum units, be they light or objects. The formula took the form of an equation not so very different from the equations that describe sound waves or harmonics or any number of things with which Isaac Newton would have been comfortable. For a brief time, physicists sought to visualize these quantum waves as ordinary waves traveling through some kind of a medium (nobody knew what kind) which somehow carried the quantum properties of an object. Then Max Born pointed out something quite astonishing: the simple interference of these quantum waves did not describe the observed behaviors; instead, the waves had to be interfered and the mathematical results of the interference had to be further manipulated (by "squaring" them, i.e., by multiplying the results by themselves) in order to achieve the final probability characteristic of all quantum events. It is a two-step process, the end result of which requires mathematical manipulation. The process cannot be duplicated by waves alone, but only by calculations based on numbers which cycled in the manner of waves.

From Born, the Schrodinger wave became known as a probability wave (although actually it is a cycling of potentialities which, when squared, yield a probability). Richard Feynman developed an elegant model for describing the amplitude (height or depth representing the relative potentiality) of the many waves involved in a quantum event, calculating the interference of all of these amplitudes, and using the final result to calculate a probability. However, Feynman disclaimed any insight into whatever physical process his system might be describing. Although his system achieved a result that was exactly and perfectly in accord with observed natural processes, to him it was nothing more than calculation. The reason was that, as far as Feynman or anybody else could tell, the underlying process itself was nothing more than calculation.

The Second Computer Analogy. A process that produces a result based on nothing more than calculation is an excellent way to describe the operations of a computer program. The two-step procedure of the Schrodinger equation and the Feynman system may be impossible to duplicate with physical systems, but for the computer it is trivial. That is what a computer does -- it manipulates numbers and calculates. (As we will discuss later, the computer must then interpret and display the result to imbue it with meaning that can be conveyed to the user.)

Wave summary. Quantum mechanics involves "waves" which cannot be duplicated or even approximated physically; but which easily can be calculated by mathematical formula and stored in memory, creating in effect a static map of the wave shape. This quality of something having the appearance and effect of a wave, but not the nature of a wave, is pervasive in quantum mechanics, and so is fundamental to all things in our universe. It is also an example of how things which are inexplicable in physical terms turn out to be necessary or convenient qualities of computer operations.

II. The Measurement Effect

A. "Collapse of the wave function" -- consciousness as mediator, as though the sensory universe was a display to the user

During the course of an observation of a quantum event, the wave-like nature of the quantum unit is not observed. The evidence for the existence of quantum waves is entirely inferential, derived from such phenomena as the interference pattern on Mr. Young's projection screen. After analyzing such a phenomenon, the conclusion is that the only thing that could cause such a pattern is a wave. ("It is as if two waves were interfering.") However, actual observation always reveals instead a particle. For example, as instruments were improved, it turned out that the interference pattern observed by Young was created not by a constant sloshing against the projection screen, but by one little hit at a time, randomly appearing at the projection screen in such a way that over time the interference pattern built up. "Particles" of light were being observed as they struck the projection screen; but the eventual pattern appeared to the eye, and from mathematical analysis, to result from a wave

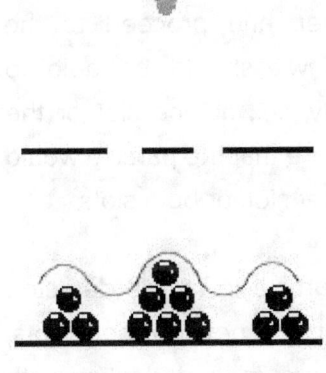

This presents conceptual difficulties that are almost insurmountable as we attempt to visualize a light bulb (or laser or electron gun) emitting a particle at the source location, which immediately dissolves into a wave as it travels through the double slits, and which then reconstitutes itself into a particle at the projection screen, usually at a place where the (presumed)

overlapping wave fronts radiating from the two slits reinforce each other. What is more, this is only the beginning of the conceptual difficulties with this phenomenon.

Investigating the mechanics of this process turns out to be impossible, for the reason that whenever we try to observe or otherwise detect a wave we obtain, instead, a particle. The very act of observation appears to change the nature of the quantum unit, according to conventional analysis. Variations on the double slit experiment provide the starkest illustration.

If we assume that quantum units are particles, it follows that the particle must travel from the emission source, through one slot or the other, and proceed to the projection screen. Therefore, we should be able to detect the particle mid-journey, i.e., at one slot or the other. The rational possibilities are that the particle would be detected at one slot, the other slot, or both slots.

Experiment shows that the particle in fact is detected always at one slot or the other slot, never at both slots, seeming to confirm that we are indeed dealing with particles.

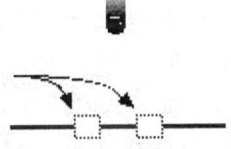

———————— 'However, a most mysterious thing happens when we detect these particles at the slots: the interference patterns disappears and is replaced by a clumping in line with the source and the slots. Thus, if we thought that some type of wave was traveling through this space in the absence of observation, we find instead a true particle upon observation -- a particle which behaves just like a particle is supposed to behave, to the point even of traveling in straight lines like a billiard ball.

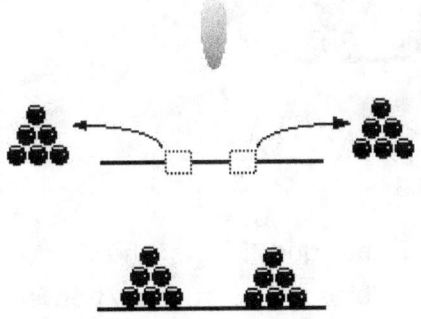

Results if electrons are detected at the slots

To further increase the mystery, it appears that the change from wave to particle takes place not upon mechanical interaction with the detecting device, but upon a conscious being's acquiring the knowledge of the results of the attempt at detection. Although not entirely free from doubt, experiment seems to indicate that the same experimental set up will yield different results (clumping pattern or interference pattern at the projection screen) depending entirely on whether the experimenter chooses to learn the results of the detection at the slits or not. This inexplicable change in behavior has been called the central mystery of quantum mechanics.

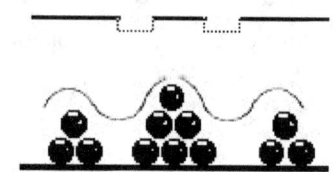

Results if electrons are NOT detected at the slots.

At the scientific level, the question is "how?" The conventional way of describing the discrepancy between analysis and observation is to say that the "wave function" is somehow "collapsed" during observation, yielding a "particle" with measurable properties. The mechanism of this transformation is completely unknown and, because the scientifically indispensable act of observation itself changes the result, it appears to be intrinsically and literally unknowable.

At the philosophical level, the question is "why?" Why should our acquisition of knowledge affect something which, to our way of thinking, should exist in whatever form it exists whether or not it is observed? Is there something special about consciousness that relates directly to the things of which we are conscious? If so, why should that be?

The computer analogy. As John Gribbin puts it, "nature seems to 'make the calculation' and then present us with an observed event."Both the "how" and the "why" of this process can be addressed through the metaphor of a computer which is programmed to project images to create an experience for the user, who is a conscious being.

The "how" is described structurally by a computer which runs a program. The program provides an algorithm for determining the position (in this example) of every part of the image, which is to say, every pixel that will be projected to the user. The mechanism for transforming the programming into the projection is the user interface. This can be analogized to the computer monitor, and the mouse or joystick or other device for viewing one part of the image or another. When the user chooses to view one part of the image, those pixels must be calculated and displayed; all other parts of the image remain stored

224

in the computer as programming. Thus, the pixels being viewed must follow the logic of the projection, which is that they should move like particles across the screen. The programming representing the parts of the image not being displayed need not follow this logic, and may remain as formulas. Calculating and displaying any particular pixel is entirely a function of conveying information to the user, and it necessarily involves a "change" from the inchoate mathematical relationships represented by the formula to the specific pixels generated according to those relationships. The user can never "see" the programming, but by analysis can deduce its mathematical operation by careful observation of the manner in which the pixels are displayed. The algorithm does not collapse into a pixel; rather, the algorithm tells the monitor where and how to produce the pixel for display to the user according to which part of the image the user is viewing.

The "why" is problematical in the cosmic sense, but is easily stated within the limits of our computer metaphor. The programming produces images for the user because the entire set up was designed to do just that: to present images to a user (viewer) as needed by the user. The ultimate "why" depends on the motivation of the designer. In our experience, the maker of a video game seeks to engage the attention of the user to the end that the user will spend money for the product and generate profits for the designer. This seems an unlikely motivation for designing the universe simulation in which we work and play.

B. Uncertainty and complementary properties, as though variables were being redefined and results calculated and recalculated according to an underlying formula

We have seen one aspect of the measurement effect, which is that measurement (or observation) appears to determine whether a quantum unit is displayed or projected to the user (as a "particle"), or whether instead the phenomenon remains inchoate, unobserved, behaving according to a mathematical algorithm (as a "wave"). There is another aspect of measurement that

relates to the observed properties of the particle-like phenomenon as it is detected. This is the famous Heisenberg uncertainty principle.

As with all aspects of quantum mechanics, the uncertainty principle is not a statement of philosophy, but rather a mathematical model which is exacting and precise. That is, we can be certain of many quantum measurements in many situations, and we can be completely certain that our results will conform to quantum mechanical principles. In quantum mechanics, the "uncertainty principle" has a specific meaning, and it describes the relationship between two properties which are "complementary," that is, which are linked in a quantum mechanical sense (they "complement" each other, i.e., they are counterparts, each of which makes the other "complete").

The original example of complementary properties was

the relationship between position and momentum. According to classical Newtonian physics and to common sense, if an object simply exists we should be able to measure both where it is and how fast it is moving. Measuring these two properties would allow us to predict where the object will be in the future. In practice, it turns out that both position and momentum cannot be exactly determined at the same moment -- a discovery that threw a monkey wrench into the clockwork predictability of the universe. Put simply, the uncertainty relationship is this: for any two complementary properties, any increase in the certainty of knowledge of one property will necessarily lead to a decrease in the certainty of knowledge of the other property.

The uncertainty principle was originally thought to be more statement of experimental error than an actual principle of any great importance. When scientists were measuring the location and the speed (or, more precisely, the momentum) of a quantum unit -- two properties which turn out to be complementary -- they found that they could not pin down both at once. That is, after measuring momentum, they would determine position; but then they found that the momentum had changed. The obvious explanation was that, in determining position, they had bumped the quantum unit and thereby changed its momentum. What they needed (so they thought) were better, less intrusive instruments. On closer inspection, however, this did not turn out to be the case. The measurements did not reliable pregnancy test are positive, you know so much change the momentum, as they made the everything there is to know about her pregnancy momentum less certain, less predictable. On remeasure- property: she is pregnant. For a "complementary" ment, the momentum might be the same, faster, or property to pregnancy, let us use marital status. (In slower. What is more, the range of uncertainty of law, you are either married or not married, with momentum increased in direct proportion to the important consequences for bigamy prosecutions.) accuracy of the measurement of location. The logical consequence of knowing everything

In 1925, Werner Heisenberg conducted a mathematical analysis of the position and momentum of quantum nature, we then would know nothing about the other units. His results were surprising, in that they showed a complementary property. For our example, we must mathematical incompatibility between the two imagine that, by learning whether a married woman is properties. Heisenberg was able to state that there was a pregnant, we thereby no longer know whether she is mathematical relationship between the properties p married. We don't forget what we once knew; we just (position) and m (momentum), such that the more can no longer be certain that we will get any particular precise your knowledge of the one, the less precise your answer the next time we check on her marital status. knowledge of the other. This "uncertainty" followed a The mathematical statement is that, by knowing formula which, itself, was quite certain. Heisenberg's pregnancy, you do not know whether she is married; mathematical formula accounted for the experimental and, by knowing marital status, you do not know results far, far more accurately than any notion of whether she is pregnant. In order to make this statement needing better equipment in the laboratory. It seems, true, if you once know her marital status, and you then then, that uncertainty in the knowledge of two learn her pregnancy status (without having you forget complementary properties is more than a laboratory your prior knowledge of marital status), the very fact of phenomenon -- it is a law of nature which can be her marital status must become random yes or no. A expressed mathematically.

complementary properties other sensory) form, it is far easier to conceive of how which are themselves quantized, the result is stark. the uncertainty principle might work. The "properties" Think about it. If a property is quantized, it can only be we measure are variables which are computed for the one way or the other; therefore, if we know anything purpose of display, which is to say, for the purpose of about this property, we know everything about this giving the user knowledge via the interface. A property.

A good way to understand the uncertainty principle is to take the extreme cases. As we will discuss later on, a distinguishing feature of quantum units is that many of their properties come in whole units and whole units only. That is, many quantum properties have an either/or quality such that there is no in between: the quantum unit must be either one way or the other. We say that these properties are "quantized," meaning that the property must be one specific value (quantity) or another, but never anything else. When the uncertainty principle is applied to two complementary properties which are themselves quantized, the result is stark. Think about it. If a property is quantized, it can only be one way or the other; therefore, if we know anything about this property, we know everything about this property.

There are few, if any, properties in our day to day lives that can be only one way or the other, never in between. If we leave aside all quibbling, we might suggest the folk wisdom that "you can't be a little bit pregnant." A woman either is pregnant, or she is not pregnant. Therefore, if you know that the results of a reliable pregnancy test are positive, you know everything there is to know about her pregnancy property: she is pregnant. For a "complementary" property to pregnancy, let us use marital status. (In law, you are either married or not married, with important consequences for bigamy prosecutions.)

The logical consequence of knowing everything about one complementary property is that, as a law of nature, we then would know nothing about the other complementary property. For our example, we must imagine that, by learning whether a married woman is pregnant, we thereby no longer know whether she is married. We don't forget what we once knew; we just can no longer be certain that we will get any particular answer the next time we check on her marital status. The mathematical statement is that, by knowing pregnancy, you do not know whether she is married; and, by

230

knowing marital status, you do not know whether she is pregnant. In order to make this statement true, if you once know her marital status, and you then learn her pregnancy status (without having you forget your prior knowledge of marital status), the very fact of her marital status must become random yes or no. A definite maybe.

What is controlling is your state of certainty about one property or the other. In just this way, the experimentalist sees an electron or some other quantum unit whose properties depend on the experimentalist's knowledge or certainty of some other complementary property.

A computer's data. If we cease to think of the quantum unit as a "thing," and begin to imagine it as a pixel, that is, as a display of information in graphic (or other sensory) form, it is far easier to conceive of how the uncertainty principle might work. The "properties" we measure are variables which are computed for the purpose of display, which is to say, for the purpose of giving the user knowledge via the Interface. A computed variable will display according to the underlying algorithm each time it is computed, and while the algorithm remains stable, the results of a particular calculation can be made to depend on some other factor, including another variable.

It would be far easier to understand our changing impressions of the hypothetical woman if we knew that, although she appeared to be a person like ourselves, in fact she was a computer projection. As a computer projection, she could be pregnant or not pregnant, married or single, according to whatever rules the computer might be using to create her image.

Complementary properties are simply paired variables, the calculation of which depends on the state of the other. Perhaps they share a memory location, so that when one variable is calculated and stored, it displaces whatever value formerly occupied that location; then the other variable would have to be calculated anew the next time it was called for. In this way, or in some analogous way, we can see that the appearance of a property does not need to be related to the previously displayed value of the property, but only to the underlying algorithm.

III. The Identical/ Interchangeable Nature of "Particles" and Measured Properties.

As though the "particles" were merely pictures of particles, like computer icons.

Quantum units of the same type are identical. Every electron is exactly the same as every other electron; every photon the same as every other photon; etc. How identical are they? So identical that Feynman was able seriously to propose that all the electrons and positrons in the universe actually are the same electron/positron, which merely has zipped back and forth in time so often that we observe it once for each of the billions of times it crosses our own time, so it seems like we are seeing billions of electrons.3 If you were to study an individual quantum unit from a collection, you would find nothing to distinguish it from any other quantum unit of the same type. Nothing whatsoever. Upon regrouping the quantum units, you could not, even in principle, distinguish which was the unit you had been studying and which was another.

The complete and utter sameness of each electron (or other quantum unit) has a number of consequences in physics. If the mathematical formula describing one electron is the same as that describing another electron, then there is no method, even in principle, of telling which is which. This means, for example, that if you begin with two quantum electrons at positions A and B, and move them to positions C and D, you cannot state whether they traveled the paths A to C and B to D, or A to D and B to C. In such a situation, there is no way to identify the electron at an end position with one or the other of the electrons at a beginning position; therefore, you must allow for the possibility that each electron at A and B arrived at either C or D. This impacts on the math predicting what will happen in any given quantum situation and, as it turns out, the final probabilities agree with this interchangeable state of affairs.

The computer analogy. Roger Penrose has likened this sameness to the images produced by a computer.4 Imagine the letter "t." On the page you are viewing, the letter "t" appears many times. Every letter t is exactly like every other letter t. That is because on a computer, the letter t is produced by displaying a

particular set of pixels on the screen. You could not, even in principle, tell one from the other because each is the identical image of a letter t. The formula for this image is buried in many layers of subroutines for displaying pixels, and the image does not change regardless of whether it is called upon to form part of the word "mathematical" or "marital".

Similarly, an electron does not change regardless of whether it is one of the two electrons associated with the helium atom, or one of the ninety-two electrons associated with the uranium atom. You could not, even in principle, tell one from another. The only way in this world to create such identical images is to use the same formula to produce the same image, over and over again whenever a display of the image is called for.

IV. Continuity and Discontinuity in Observed Behaviors

A. "Quantum leaps," as though there was no time or space between quantum events

In our experience, things move from one end to the other by going through the middle; they get from cold to hot by going through warm; they get from slow to fast by going through medium; and so on. Phenomena move from a lower state to a higher state in a ramp-like fashion --

continuously increasing until they reach the higher state. Even if the transition is quick, it still goes through all of the intermediate states before reaching the new, higher state.

In quantum mechanics, however, there is no transition at all. Electrons are in a low energy state on one observation, and in a higher energy state on the next; they spin one way at first, and in the opposite direction next. The processes proceed step-wise; but more than step-wise, there is no time or space in which the process exists in any intermediate state.

It is a difficult intellectual challenge to imagine a physical object that can change from one form into another form, or move from one place to another place, without going through any transition between the two states. Zeno's paradoxes offer a rigorously logical examination of this concept, with results that have frustrated analysts for millennia.5 In brief, Zeno appears to have "proved" that motion is not possible, because continuity (smooth transitions) between one state and the next implies an infinite number of transitions to accomplish any change whatsoever. Zeno's paradoxes imply that space and time are discontinuous -- discrete points and discrete instants with nothing in between, not even nothing. Yet the mind reels to imagine space and time as disconnected, always seeking to understand what lies between two points or two instants which are said to be separate.

The pre-computer analogy. Before computer animation there was the motion picture. Imagine that you are watching a movie. The motion on the screen appears to be smooth and continuous. Now, the projectionist begins to slow the projection rate. At

some point, you begin to notice a certain jerkiness in the picture. As the projection rate slows, the jerkiness increases, and you are able to focus on one frame of the movie, followed by a blanking of the screen, followed by the next frame of the movie. Eventually, you see that the motion which seemed so smooth and continuous when projected at 30 frames per second or so is really only a series of still shots. There is no motion in any of the pictures, yet by rapidly flashing a series of pictures depicting intermediate positions of an actor or object, the effective illusion is one of motion.

The computer analogy. Computers create images in the same manner. First, they compose a still image and project it; then they compose the next still image and project that one. If the computer is quick enough, you do not notice any transition. Nevertheless, the computer's "time" is completely discrete, discontinuous, and digital. One step at a time.

Similarly, the computer's "space" is discrete, discontinuous, and digital. If you look closely at a computer monitor, you notice that it consists of millions of tiny dots, nothing more. A beautifully rendered image is made up of these dots.

The theory and architecture of computers lend themselves to a step-by-step approach to any and all problems. It appears that there is no presently conceived computer architecture that would allow anything but such a discrete, digitized time and space, controlled by the computer's internal clock ticking one operation at a time. Accordingly, it seems that this lack of continuity, so bizarre and puzzling as a feature of our natural world, is an inherent characteristic of a computer simulation.

B.   *The breakdown at zero, yielding infinities, as though the universe was being run by a computer clock on a coordinate grid*

Quantum theory assumes that space and time are continuous. This is simply an assumption, not a necessary part of the theory. However, this assumption has raised some difficulties when performing calculations of quantum mechanical phenomena. Chief among these is the recurring problem of infinities.

In quantum theory, all quantum units which appear for the purpose of measurement are conceived of as dimensionless points. These are assigned a place on the coordinate grid, described by the three numbers of height, depth, and width as we have seen, but they are assigned only these three numbers. By contrast, if you consider any physical object, it will have some size, which is to say it will have its own height, width, and depth. If you were to exactly place such a physical object, you would have to take into account its own size, and to do so you would have to assign coordinates to each edge of the object.

When physicists consider quantum units as particles, there does not seem to be any easy way to determine their outer edges, if, in fact, they have any outer edges. Accordingly, quantum "particles" are designated as simple points, without size and, therefore, without edges. The three coordinate numbers are then sufficient to locate such a pointlike particle at a single point in space.

The difficulty arises when the highly precise quantum calculations are carried out all the way down to an actual zero distance (which is the size of a dimensionless point -- zero height, zero width, zero depth). At that point [sic], the quantum equations return a result of infinity, which is as meaningless to the physicist as it is to the philosopher. This result gave physicists fits for some twenty years (which is not really so long when you consider that the same problem had been giving philosophers fits for some twenty-odd centuries). The quantum mechanical solution was made possible when it was discovered that the infinities disappeared if one stopped at some arbitrarily small distance -- say, a billionth-of-a-billionth-of-a-billionth of an inch -- instead of proceeding all the way to an actual zero. One problem remained, however, and that was that there was no principled way to determine where one should stop. One physicist might stop at a billionth-of-a-billionth-of-a-billionth of an inch, and another might stop at only a thousandth-of-a-billionth-of-a-billionth of an inch. The infinities disappeared either way. The only requirement was to stop somewhere short of the actual zero point. It seemed much too arbitrary. Nevertheless, this mathematical quirk eventually gave physicists a method for doing their calculations according to a process called "renormalization," which allowed them to keep their

assumption that an actual zero point exists, while balancing one positive infinity with another negative infinity in such a way that all of the infinities cancel each other out, leaving a definite, useful number.

In a strictly philosophical mode, we might suggest that all of this is nothing more than a revisitation of Zeno's Achilles paradox of dividing space down to infinity. The philosophers couldn't do it, and neither can the physicists. For the philosopher, the solution of an arbitrarily small unit of distance -- any arbitrarily small unit of distance -- is sufficient for the resolution of the paradox. For the physicist, however, there should appear some reason for choosing one small distance over another. None of the theoretical models have presented any compelling reason for choosing any particular model as the "quantum of length." Because no such reason appears, the physicist resorts to the "renormalization" process, which is profoundly dissatisfying to both philosopher and physicist. Richard Feynman, who won a Nobel prize for developing the renormalization process, himself describes the procedure as "dippy" and "hocus-pocus." The need to resort to such a mathematical sleight-of-hand to obtain meaningful results in quantum calculations is frequently cited as the most convincing piece of evidence that quantum theory -- for all its precision and ubiquitous application

• is somehow lacking, somehow missing something. It may be that one missing element is quantized space -- a shortest distance below which there is no space, and below which one need not calculate. The arbitrariness of choosing the distance would be no more of a theoretical problem than the arbitrariness of the other fundamental constants of nature -- the speed of light, the quantum of action, and the gravitational constant. None of these can be derived from theory, but are simply observed to be constant values. Alas, this argument will not be settled until we can make far more accurate measurements than are possible today.

Quantum time. If space is quantized, then time almost surely must be quantized also. This relationship is implied by the theory of relativity, which supposes that time and space are so interrelated as to be practically the same thing. Thus, relativity is most commonly understood to imply that space and time cannot be thought of in isolation from each other; rather, we must analyze our world in terms of a single concept -- "space-time." Although the theory of relativity is largely outside the scope of this essay, the reader can see from Zeno's paradoxes how space and time are intimately related in the analysis of motion. For the moment, I will only note that the theory of relativity significantly extends this view, to the point where space and time may be considered two sides of the same coin.

The idea of "quantized" time has the intellectual virtue of consistency within the framework of quantum mechanics. That is, if the energies of electron units are quantized, and the wavelengths of light are quantized, and so many other phenomena are quantized, why not space and time? Isn't it easier to imagine how the "spin" of an electron unit can change from up to down without going through anything in the middle if we assume a quantized time? With quantized time, we may imagine that the change in such an either/or property takes place in one unit of time, and that, therefore, there is no "time" at which the spin is anywhere in the middle. Without quantized time, it is far more difficult to eliminate the intervening spin directions.

Nevertheless, the idea that time (as well as space) is "quantized," i.e., that time comes in individual units, is still controversial. The concept has been seriously proposed on many occasions, but most current scientific theories do not depend on the nature of time in this sense. About all scientists can say is that if time is not continuous, then the changes are taking place too rapidly to measure, and too rapidly to make any detectable difference in any experiment that they have dreamed up. The theoretical work that has been done on the assumption that time may consist of discontinuous jumps often focuses on the most plausible scale, which is related to the three fundamental constants of nature -- the speed of light, the quantum of action, and the gravitational constant. This is sometimes called the "Planck scale," involving the "Planck time," after the German physicist Max Planck, who laid much of the foundation of quantum mechanics through his study of minimum units in nature. On this theoretical basis, the pace of time would be around 10-44 seconds. That is one billionth-of-a-billionth-of-a-billionth-of-a-billionth of a second. And that is much too quick to measure by today's methods, or by any method that today's scientists are able to conceive of, or even hope for.

Mixing philosophy, science, time, and space. We see that the branch of physics known as relativity has been remarkably successful in its conclusion that space and time are two sides of the same coin, and should properly be thought of as a single entity: space-time. We see also that the philosophical logic of Zeno's paradoxes has always strongly implied that both space and time are quantized at some smallest, irreducible level, but that this conclusion has long been resisted because it did not seem to agree with human experience in the "real world." Further, we see that quantum mechanics has both discovered the ancient paradoxes anew in its mathematics, and provided some evidence of quantized space and time in its essential experimental results showing that "physical" processes jump from one state to the next without transition. The most plausible conclusion to be drawn from all of this is that space and time are, indeed, quantized. That is, there is some unit of distance or length which can be called "1," and which admits no fractions; and, similarly, there is some unit of time which can be called "1," and which also admits no fractions.

Although most of the foregoing is mere argument, it is compelling in its totality, and it is elegant in its power to resolve riddles both ancient and modern. Moreover, if we accept the quantization of space and time as a basic fact of the structure of our universe, then we may go on to consider how both of these properties happen to be intrinsic to the operations of a computer, as discussed above at Point IV(A).

V. Non-locality

As though all calculations were in the CPU, regardless of the location of the pixels on the screen.

A second key issue in quantum mechanics is the phenomenon of connectedness -- the ancient concept that all things are one -- because science has come increasingly to espouse theories that are uncannily related to this notion. In physics, this phenomenon is referred to as non-locality.

The essence of a local interaction is direct contact -- as basic as a punch in the nose. Body A affects body B locally when it either touches B or touches something else that touches B. A gear train is a typical local mechanism. Motion passes from one gear wheel to another in an unbroken chain. Break the chain by taking out a single gear and the movement cannot continue. Without something there to mediate it, a local interaction cannot cross a gap.

On the other hand, the essence of non-locality is unmediated action-at-a-distance. A non-local interaction jumps from body A to body B without touching anything in between. Voodoo injury is an example of a non-local interaction. When a voodoo practitioner sticks a pin in her doll, the distant target is (supposedly) instantly wounded, although nothing actually travels from doll to victim. Believers in voodoo claim that an action here causes an effect there; that's all there is to it. Without benefit of mediation, a non-local interaction effortlessly flashes across the void.6

Even "flashes across the void" is a bit misleading, because "flashing" implies movement, however quick, and "across" implies distance traveled, however empty. In fact, non-locality simply does away with speed and distance, so that the cause and effect simply happen. Contrary to common sense or scientific sensibility, it appears that under certain circumstances an action here on earth can have immediate consequences across the world, or on another star, or clear across the universe. There is no apparent transfer of energy at any speed, only an action here and a consequence there.

Non-locality for certain quantum events was theorized in the 1930s as a result of the math. Many years were wasted (by Einstein, among others) arguing that such a result was absurd and could not happen regardless of what the math said. In the 1960s, the theory was given a rigorous mathematical treatment by John S. Bell, who showed that if quantum effects were "local" they would result in one statistical distribution, and if "non-local" in another distribution. In the 1970s and '80s, the phenomenon was demonstrated, based on Bell's theorem, by the actual statistical distribution of experiments. For those die-hard skeptics who distrust statistical proofs, the phenomenon appears recently to have been demonstrated directly at the University of Innsbruck.7

More than any of the bizarre quantum phenomena observed since 1900, the phenomenon of non-locality caused some serious thought to be given to the question, "What is reality?" The question had been nagging since the 1920s, when the Copenhagen school asserted, essentially, that our conception of reality had to stop with what we could observe; deeper than that we could not delve and, therefore, we could never determine experimentally why we observe what we observe. The experimental proof of non-locality added nothing to this strange statement, but seemed to force the issue. The feeling was that if our side of the universe could affect the other side of the universe, then those two widely separated places must somehow be connected. Alternative explanations necessarily involved signals traveling backward in time so that the effect "causes the cause," which seemed far too contrived for most scientists' tastes. Accordingly, it was fair to ask whether apparent separations in space and time -- I'm in the living room, you're in the den -- are fundamentally "real"; or whether, instead, they are somehow an illusion, masking a deeper reality in which all things are one, sitting right on top of each other, always connected one to another and to all. This sounds suspiciously like mysticism, and the similarity of scientific and mystical concepts led to some attempts to import Eastern philosophy into Western science. Zukav, in particular, wants desperately to find a direct connection between science and Buddhism, but he would concede that the link remains to be discovered.

Note that the experimental results had been predicted on the basis of the mathematical formalism of quantum mechanics, and not from any prior experiments. That is, the formal mathematical description of two quantum units in certain circumstances implied that their properties thereafter would be connected regardless of separation in space or time (just as $x + 2 = 4$ implies that $x = 2$). It then turned out that these properties are connected regardless of separation in space or time. The experimentalists in the laboratory had confirmed that where the math can be manipulated to produce an absurd result, the matter and energy all around us obligingly will be found to behave in exactly that absurd manner. In the case of non-locality, the behavior is uncomfortably close to magic.

The computer analogy. The non-locality which appears to be a basic feature of our world also finds an analogy in the same metaphor of a computer simulation. In terms of cosmology, the scientific question is, "How can two particles separated by half a universe be understood as connected such that they interact as though they were right on top of each other?" If we analogize to a computer simulation, the question would be, "How can two pictures at the far corners of the screen be understood as connected such that the distance between them is irrelevant?"

In fact, the measured distance between any two pixels (dots) on the monitor's display turns out to be entirely irrelevant, since both are merely the products of calculations carried out in the bowels of the computer as directed by the programming. The pixels may be as widely separated as you like, but the programming generating them is forever embedded in the computer's memory in such a way that -- again speaking quite literally -- the very concept of separation in space and time of the pixels has no meaning whatsoever for the stored information

VI. The Relationship of Observed Phenomena to the Mathematical Formalism

As though physical manifestations themselves were being produced by a mathematical formula.

Perhaps the most striking aspect of quantum theory is the relationship of all things to the math, as with the phenomenon of non-locality discussed above, which occurs in nature, so it seems, because that is the way the equations calculate. Even though the mathematical formulas were initially developed to describe the behavior of universe, these formulas turn out to govern the behavior of the universe with an exactitude that defies our concept of mathematics. As Nick Herbert puts it, "Whatever the math does on paper, the Quantum stuff does in the outside world." That is, if the math can be manipulated to produce some absurd result, it will always turn out that the matter and energy around us actually behave in exactly that absurd manner when we look closely enough. It is as though our universe is being produced by the mathematical formulas. The backwards logic implied by quantum mechanics, where the mathematical formalism seems to be more "real" than the things and objects of nature, is unavoidable. In any conceptual conflict between what a mathematical equation can obtain for a result, and what a real object actually could do, the quantum mechanical experimental results always will conform to the mathematical prediction.

Quantum theory is rooted in statistics, and such reality conflicts often arise in statistics. For example, the math might show that a "statistically average" American family has **2.13** children, even though we know that a family of real human beings must have a whole number of children. In our experience, we would never find such a statistically average family regardless of the math, because there simply is no such thing as 13/100ths of a child. The math is entirely valid, but it must yield to the census-taker's whole-child count when we get down to examining individual families. In quantum mechanics, however, the math will prevail -- as though the statistics were drawn up in advance and all American families were created equally with exactly 2.13 children, nevermind that we cannot begin to conceive of such a family. To the mathematician, these two situations are equivalent, because either way the average American family ends up with 2.13 children. But the quantum mechanical relationship of the math to the observation does not make any sense to us because in our world view, numbers are just symbols representing something with independent existence.

Mr. Herbert states that, "Quantum theory is a method of representing quantum stuff mathematically: a model of the world executed in symbols."9 Since quantum theory describes the world perfectly -- so perfectly that its symbolic, mathematical predictions always prevail over physical insight -- the equivalence between quantum symbolism and universal reality must be more than an oddity: it must be the very nature of reality.

This is the point at which we lose our nerve; yet the task for the Western rationalist is to find a mechanical model from our experience corresponding to a "world executed in symbols."

The final computer analogy. An example which

literally fits this description is the computer simulation, which is a graphic representation created by executing programming code. The programming code itself consists of nothing but symbols, such as 0 and 1. Numbers, text, graphics and anything else you please are coded by unique series of numbers. These symbolic codes have no meaning in themselves, but arbitrarily are assigned values which have significance according to the operations of the computer. The symbols are manipulated according to the various step-by-step sequences (algorithms) by which the programming instructs the computer how to create the graphic representation. The picture presented on-screen to the user is a world executed in colored dots; the computer's programming is a world (the same world) executed in symbols. Anyone who has experienced a computer crash knows that the programming (good or bad) governs the picture, and not vice versa. All of this forms a remarkably tight analogy to the relationship between the quantum math on paper, and the behavior of the "quantumstuff" in the outside world.

The epistemology of universe creation on a computer

F.J.Tipler has suggested that our universe could be a computer program running on a computer in another universe, (see, for example, p240-244 of Tipler 1989, and p206-209 of Tipler 1995). Tipler imagines a perfect computer simulation of our universe, which precisely matches the evolution in time of our own universe, and precisely represents every property of every entity in our universe. Such a simulation would simulate all the people who exist in our own universe. Such simulated people,

255

suggests Tipler, would reflect upon the fact that they think, would interact with their apparent environment, and would conclude that they exist. Their experience would be indistinguishable from our own experience, and Tipler infers from this that we ourselves cannot know that we are not part of such a computer program. Ex hypothesi, there is nothing in our experience which could be evidence that we are not part of such a program, hence, it might be argued, we cannot know that we are not part of a computer program.

This argument is a type of epistemological scepticism, similar to Descartes' dreaming argument. Descartes raised the possibility that one could experience a dream which is indistinguishable from the experience of a conscious, waking individual. The sceptical argument from this is that, ex hypothesi, there is nothing in one's experience which could be evidence that one is not dreaming, hence one cannot know that one is not dreaming.

A modern version of this is the 'brain in a vat' hypothesis. Jonathan Dancy characterises this sceptical hypothesis as follows: "You do not know that you are not a brain in a vat full of liquid in a laboratory, and wired to a computer which is feeding you your current experiences under the control of some ingenious technician/scientist...For if you were such a brain, then, provided that the scientist is successful, nothing in your experience could possibly reveal that you were; for your experience is ex hypothesi identical with that of something which is not a brain in a vat. Since you have only your own experience to appeal to, and that experience is the same in either situation, nothing can reveal to you which situation is the actual one," (Dancy 1985, p10).

One can identify two distinct premises in this argument:

(a). It is possible for a brain in a vat to be fed experience of an illusional world.

(b). It is possible for that experience to be indistinguishable from our own experience.

From these premises, the reasoning is as follows: Because the experience of the illusional world would be indistinguishable from one's own experience, it is not possible to know whether or not one's own experience is experience of a real world, or experience of an illusional world fed to a brain in a vat. Hence, it is not possible to know whether or not one is a brain in a vat.

There is, however, a vital ambiguity in the argument. There are two different senses in which real world experience could be indistinguishable from illusional world experience. One could claim either of the following two propositions:

1. The experience of the illusional world would be indistinguishable from the real world in terms of the detailed content of the experience.

2. The experience of the illusional world would be indistinguishable as experience from experience of the real world. In other words, the form of the illusory experience would be indistinguishable from the form of real-world experience.

It is not clear which of these claims Dancy is making. To illustrate the differences between these claims, consider the following scenarios:

Firstly, suppose that an individual is born in the real world, grows-up in the real world, and experiences the real world for 30 years, developing a range of cognitive skills, and accumulating a large collection of memories. Then, one night, whilst he lies asleep, the individual is unknowingly drugged and kidnapped by a scientist. As the victim lies unconscious in the scientist's laboratory, his brain is removed and wired up to a computer. When the individual is allowed to recover consciousness, he wakes up to experience an illusional world controlled by the computer. Suppose that the individual retains his memories of the real world. To prevent the individual from having a reason to believe that he is a brain in a vat, the experience of the illusional world must be indistinguishable from the individual's experience of the real world. Both the form and the detailed content of the individual's illusory experience must be indistinguishable from his experience of the real world. The illusional world must have the same spatial layout and the same apparent history as that part of the real world known to the victim, and the illusional world must evolve according to the same laws that operate in the real world. The victim must feel that he experiences his world, and influences events in his world, with the same body that he possessed before he fell asleep the previous night. The victim must not recognize any difference between the real world and the illusional world that is not explicable by the laws of the real world. The victim must appear to perceive the same world he perceived before he fell asleep the previous night.

If these conditions were satisfied, then the individual would have no justification for believing that he is a brain in a vat. In accordance with conventional definitions of knowledge, if the individual would not be justified in believing that he is a brain in a vat, then he could not know that he is a brain in a vat.

It is possible to imagine other sceptical scenarios which do not require the detailed nature of the illusional world to be indistinguishable from the detailed nature of the real world. If an individual's memories of the real world are deleted or suppressed, and apparent memories of an illusional world completely different from the real world are added, then experience of the illusional world would not give the individual reason to believe that he experiences an illusional world. The individual could experience an illusional world with a spatial layout and history totally different to the spatial layout and history of the real world. The illusional world could operate according to laws different to those that operate in the real world. Nevertheless, the experience of the illusional world would be indistinguishable, as experience, from experience of the real world. In other words, the form of the illusory experience, if not the detailed content, would be indistinguishable from real-world experience.

To take another example, if an individual were fed illusory experiences from birth, that individual would have no memories of the real world. Hence, experience of an illusory world completely different from the real world in terms of detailed content, would not give the individual reason to believe that he experiences an illusional world.

It is not necessary to suppose that the individual who experiences an illusional world is an unwilling participant. It is possible, for example, that one's entire lifetime of experience upon 20th/21st century Earth, is part of a virtual reality game, played on a distant planet in the far-future. The technology of the far-future might enable game-players to play any role, in any factual or fictitious world. The game technology might suppress one's real-world memories, and supply the memories of the character one is playing. If the game technology suppressed one's real-world memories, one would be unaware of playing a virtual reality game. The game technology might even suppress one's real-world cognitive skills; one might experience birth, growth and mental development in the game world. Either way, one would have no memory of deciding to enter the game world. Once again, the sceptical argument is that one's own experience is indistinguishable from the experience of someone playing such a virtual reality game, hence one cannot know whether or not one is playing such a game.

Those sceptical arguments which require the detailed nature of the illusional world to be indistinguishable from the detailed nature of the real world, share a common point of vulnerability. It is possible for the hypothesis supporting such sceptical arguments to be false, and it is possible to know that it is false.

If the detailed content of the illusory experience is indistinguishable from the detailed content of real experience, then one can infer facts about the real world from one's experience, irrespective of whether one's experience is illusory or not. This allows one to determine, by scientific investigation, whether the hypothesis which supports the sceptical argument, is true or false.

For example, consider the brain in a vat argument. Recall that this sceptical argument is based upon the premise that it is possible for a brain in a vat to be fed experience of an illusional world. Because the illusional world would be indistinguishable, by hypothesis, from the real world, one's sensory systems and neurophysiology in the illusional world would be the same as one's sensory systems and neurophysiology in the real world. Hence, one could learn about one's real world physiology and neurology from one's experience, irrespective of whether one's experience is experience of the real world, or the illusional experience of a brain in a vat. One could not be led into forming false beliefs about the kind of entity one is without the violation of the indistinguishability condition.

Investigation of the human brain may reveal that it is impossible for it to be stimulated in a way which would produce experience indistinguishable from the experience of a person who is not a brain in a vat. Thus, the hypothesis upon which the sceptical argument is based, could be false. If one knew from neurophysiology that it is not possible for one to be a brain in a vat, then one would know that one is not a brain in a vat. When Dancy characterises the sceptical argument he states that "you have only your own experience to appeal to," (Dancy 1985, p10). This is false because one can also appeal to one's scientific understanding, based upon both theory and empirical evidence.

The other sceptical scenarios share this vulnerability: neurophysiological investigation of the brain could reveal that it is not possible for dreams to be indistinguishable from the experiences of a waking individual; research in micro-electronics, computer science, and human physiology, might conclude that totally authentic virtual reality is not possible.

Those sceptical arguments which do not require the detailed nature of the illusional world to be indistinguishable from the detailed nature of the real world, are more robust. If the detailed nature of the illusional world is different from the detailed nature of the real world, then one cannot necessarily learn about real world physiology and neurology from illusory experience. However, these more robust sceptical scenarios are dependent upon the following premise:

• Either it is possible to delete or suppress an individual's memories of the real world, and to replace them with apparent memories of an illusional world, or it is possible to feed an individual with illusory experience from birth.

If this premise is false, then all the sceptical arguments which concern illusional worlds might be refuted by empirical investigation. It is, however, difficult to establish whether this premise is true or false. If scientific

264

investigation reveals that it is impossible in our world to feed an individual illusory experiences from birth, and that it is impossible in our world to delete or suppress an individual's memories, and replace them with apparent memories of an illusional world, then this alone does not establish whether the premise is true or false. If our world is an illusional world, and if the detailed nature of the illusional world is different from the real world, then scientific discoveries about our world, the illusional world, do not tell us anything about the real world.

It has been assumed in this section that it is possible to make a distinction between the form and content of experience. If such a distinction is not possible, then the sceptical scenarios must be re-categorised as follows:

1. An individual in our world experiences an illusional world which is indistinguishable from experience of our world. The individual is unaware that his experience is illusional precisely because the illusional experience is indistinguishable from experience of our world.

2. An individual in our world experiences an illusional world which is distinguishable from experience of our world. The individual is unaware of the difference, either

because his memories of our world have been deleted or suppressed, or because he has experienced the illusional world from birth.

In case 1 the sceptical argument is as before, with the reference to the content of experience omitted. In case 2, the sceptical argument is as follows: If an individual in our world could experience an illusional world which is distinguishable from experience of our world, and if that individual could be made unaware that what he experiences is illusional, then our own world experience could be illusional experience, distinguishable from the real world. We cannot know whether or not our experience is experience of the real world, or experience of an illusional world different from the real world.

The computer program hypothesis differs in one respect from the brain-in-a-vat type of hypothesis. The latter hypothesis suggests that an individual in a real world could be fed experiences of an illusional world, a world that does not objectively exist. The computer program hypothesis suggests that an entire universe could be created as a computer program, and that many individuals could be created as part of the program. This hypothesis does not merely suggest that there is a computer program which is feeding illusory experiences to individuals who exist in a real world. Instead, individuals capable of experience are themselves created by the program, and the world they experience is just as real relative to them, as our world is relative to us. It is not Tipler's claim that we cannot know whether or not our world is an illusional world. Instead, he claims that "we cannot know if the universe in which we find ourselves is actually ultimate reality," (Tipler 1995, p208). Tipler's claim is that we cannot know what level of reality we experience; that we cannot know whether or not the universe we experience has been created on a computer existing in another universe.

However, the hypothesis that our own universe is indistinguishable from a universe created on a computer, may be false. It will be demonstrated in this paper that physical predictions follow from the hypothesis that our universe is a program running on a digital computer. For example, it follows that the structure of the universe must be discrete, and that the spatial universe must be compact. If these predictions are found to be false, then it is impossible for our universe to be a program running on a digital computer. If the predictions are falsified, then our universe is distinguishable from a universe created on a digital computer. Alternatively, if these predictions are found to be true, then it remains possible for our universe to be a program running on a digital computer. Empirical investigation is necessary to determine if the computer program hypothesis is possible.

• The metaphysics of universe creation on a computer

The hypothesis that our universe is a program running on a computer in another universe is not merely a sceptical epistemological hypothesis, but a metaphysical hypothesis, in the sense defined below.

The term 'metaphysics' seems to have at least two different meanings. On the one hand, it is the study of that which possibly exists beyond the physical world. On the other hand, it is a whole group of philosophical subjects, such as the studies of time, causation, substance, and universals. These subjects seem to be united by the fact that they involve very general, foundational study of the nature of things.

For the purpose of this paper, metaphysics is defined to be the study of that which possibly exists beyond the empirically detectable world. In contrast, physics is defined to be the study of the empirically detectable world. The hypothesis that our universe is a program running on a computer in another universe, is clearly a metaphysical hypothesis, in the very specific sense defined here. The hypothesis is that the computer hardware on which the program is running cannot be empirically detected by the beings represented in the software, hence the hypothesis is metaphysical rather than physical.

It is important to distinguish Tipler's hypothesis from a metaphysically distinct proposal made by J.D.Barrow. Barrow suggests that "If we were to regard the Universe as a vast computer...then we can readily envisage the laws of Nature as some form of software which runs upon the particular forms of matter that form the world of strings and elementary particles," (Barrow 1991, p160). In Tipler's computer program hypothesis, the computer hardware is inaccessible to the people represented in the computer program; the constituents of matter, elementary particles or not, are just as much a part of the program software as the laws of physics. Presumably, each different type of particle or field would correspond to a different data type in the program. Each individual particle or field would then correspond to an instance of the relevant data type. In programming parlance, an instance of a data type is called a data object. Hence, the constituents of matter would correspond to data objects defined in the program. The laws of physics would correspond to the algorithms which act upon the data objects defined in the program. In general, entities would correspond to data objects in a computer program, and processes would correspond to algorithms. For example, an individual electron would correspond to a data object, and the Dirac equation would correspond to an algorithm capable of acting upon any electron data object. To give another example, in the geometrodynamics formulation of general relativity, a 3-manifold Σ, and the tensor fields ($°i$; Ki; $\acute{A}i$) representing the intrinsic geometry $°i$, extrinsic geometry Ki, and matter fields $\acute{A}i$ at time i, would all correspond to data objects. The geometrodynamics evolution process would correspond to an algorithm which calculates ($°j+1$; $Kj +1$; $\acute{A}j+1$) from ($°j$; Kj; $\acute{A}j$).

After suggesting that our universe could be a computer program running on a computer in another universe, Tipler goes one step further, and claims that there is no need for a computer to be running the program. The state of memory of a digital computer can be treated as a long string of binary digits, and this represents a natural number in binary notation. Given that a computer program maps an initial memory state to a final memory state, a computer program can be treated as a mapping on the set of natural numbers. Tipler duly treats a program as an abstract mapping N ! N, and claims that "if time were to exist globally, and if the most basic things in

270

the physical universe and the time steps between one instant and the next were discrete," (Tipler 1995, p208), then our universe could be in one-to-one correspondence with such an abstract object. Tipler acknowledges that the most basic things in the physical universe could be continuous, hence he proposes a further generalization of what a simulation is: "Let us say that a perfect simulation exists if the physical universe can be put into one-to-one correspondence with some mutually consistent subcollection of all mathematical concepts," (ibid., p209).

This proposal does not merely suppose that mathematical Platonism is true, that mathematical objects exist independently of the physical universe, in an abstract realm. Nor does it merely suppose that physical objects possess intrinsic mathematical properties. Instead, it supposes that physical objects can be identified with mathematical objects. As Barrow puts it, "We exist in the Platonic realm," (Barrow 1992, p282). Whilst this is a fascinating idea, I shall restrict the discussion in this paper to the hypothesis that our universe is a program running on a computer in another universe.

The notion that there is something which exists beyond

the empirically detectable world has famous precedents in the history of philosophy. Various types of thing have been postulated to exist beyond the physical world: mental entities, theological entities, and mathematical entities. These types of metaphysical suggestion are of no relevance to this paper. Rather, the focus of attention is the metaphysical hypothesis that there is something non-mental, non-deistic, and non-mathematical, which exists beyond our physical world. For example, Kant proposed that there are things-in-themselves, so-called 'noumena', which exist beyond the empirically accessible world. The metaphysics of the computer program hypothesis can be compared with the metaphysics of Kant's noumena.

To recall, Kant suggested that there is a distinction between noumena and phenomena. The noumena are things in themselves, and the phenomena are the appearances of things in sensory perception. There are three possible ways of defining noumena. The noumena could be things which exist independently of sensory perception, they could be things which exist independently of empirical detectability, or they could be things which exist independently of cognition al-together. Obviously, things which exist independently of empirical detectability also exist independently of sensory perception, and things which exist independently of cognition also exist independently of empirical detectability.

If one merely stipulates that noumena are things which exist independently of sensory perception, then noumena could simply be things which are too small to see, like atoms and electrons. Things which are too small to see are still empirically detectable. As a classic example, an electron leaves a luminescent trail in a Wilson Cloud Chamber. The electron is not directly perceivable, but it is nevertheless detectable. Kant seems to suggest that noumena exist independently of both sense perception and empirical detectability of any kind. Further, Kant seems to hold that noumena are beyond cognition altogether. The computer program hypothesis holds that the states and processes of the computer in another universe, exist beyond both sense perception and empirical detectability, but these states and processes are not beyond cognition. What exists beyond the physical world is conceivable, according to the computer program hypothesis. In contrast, Kant seems to hold that we cannot even conceive what things in themselves are like.

The computer program hypothesis is consistent with a

threefold distinction between the phenomenal, the physical, and the metaphysical. This corresponds to the distinction between appearance, physical reality, and metaphysical reality. Appearances and phenomena consist of sensory experiences such as colours, sounds, and smells. Physical reality is the world described by physics, the world of atoms, electrons, and space-time. The hypothetical metaphysical reality consists of the states and processes of a computer in another universe. In this threefold distinction, space and time exist independently of sensory appearances, whereas Kant believed that space and time are merely the format into which sensory experience is arranged. Unlike Kant, the proposal in this paper will not relegate space-time to the merely phenomenal.

The computer program hypothesis is an interesting case because the global metaphysics is drawn from local physics. The nature of what lies beyond the entire physical universe (global metaphysics) is drawn from the nature of the computer, a part of the physical world (local physics).

This paper proposes that, in general, the relationship between metaphysics and physics should be similar to the relationship between topology and geometry. A particular topology constrains the possible geometry, but is, nevertheless, consistent with a range of different geometries. For example, given the topology of the n-sphere Sn, it is impossible for the geometry to be flat, but there are, nevertheless, many possible geometries on Sn with non-zero curvature. Topology has implications for geometry, but a particular topology does not entail a unique geometry. Similarly, a metaphysical theory should, at the very least, have implications for the physical world. A metaphysical model should constrain the possible physical models, but a metaphysical model should not entail a unique physical model. In general, a metaphysical model should be consistent with a range of different physical models.

Conversely, it is not possible to infer a unique topology from geometrical properties like sectional curvature. Similarly, it is not possible to infer a unique metaphysical model from a physical model. However, geometrical properties do have topological implications, and similarly, the theories of physics do have metaphysical implications.

The computer program hypothesis developed in this paper exemplifies these proposed standards for a metaphysical theory. Properly developed, the hypothesis makes predictions about the physical universe. The metaphysical hypothesis that our universe is a program running on a digital computer entails that

- The universe is discrete

- The solutions to the fundamental evolution equations of physics must be computable functions

- The spatial universe has compact topology

These predictions are empirically testable, hence the metaphysical computer program hypothesis is empirically testable. It will be demonstrated that the computer program hypothesis might be verifiable or falsifiable by astronomical observation. None of the predictions above will be invalidated by the devel-opment of quantum computers. Although quantum computers might be able to perform certain calculations faster than computers based upon the notion of a Turing machine, the collection of uncomputable functions for a quantum computer is the same as the collection of uncomputable functions for a Tur-ing machine. Like existing computers, quantum computers will possess a finite memory. And like existing digital computers, a quantum computer will only be able to represent discrete things.

Not only should a metaphysical hypothesis or theory have physical implications, but it should be formulated with the precise concepts provided by mathematics, just like a physical hypothesis or theory. There is no reason why natural language should be adequate in metaphysics when it is inadequate in physics. The meanings of the terms in mathematics are precisely established with stipulative definitions. In contrast, the meanings of the terms in natural language are often determined by use, and the use is inconsistent amongst the community of language users. If use determines meaning, and use is inconsistent, then it follows that meaning is ambiguous. Use varies from one member of the community to another, and use changes over time, hence if use determines meaning, then meanings vary from one member of the community to another, and meanings change over time.2 This makes natural language inadequate if precision is sought.

If one defines metaphysics as the study of that which possibly exists beyond the empirically detectable world, there is nothing in that definition which entails that physics cannot have any metaphysical implications, or vice versa, and there is nothing in that definition which entails that mathematics cannot be used to formulate metaphysical theories. It would be strange indeed if a discipline were defined not by its subject matter, but by the methodological tools contingently used at one time to study that subject matter. If metaphysics were defined to be the natural language study of that which possibly exists beyond the empirically detectable world, it would be rather like an architect who refuses to use Computer Aided Design tools because he has defined architectural design to be a matter of pen and paper alone. If the pursuit of knowledge is one's main objective, then one uses every conceptual resource at one's disposal.

Kant's metaphysics provides a good example of what is wrong with traditional metaphysics. His principal metaphysical assertion is that there are things-in-themselves, so-called 'noumena', which exist beyond the empirically accessible world. Although Kant seems to resist claiming that noumena cause phenomena, he does believe that phenomena are dependent in some way upon noumena. However, he also claims that the noumena are unknowable. If there are things-in-themselves, the noumena, and if they do have some relationship to phenomena, then any well-developed, detailed speculation about the nature of the noumena must have testable predictions about phenomena. Only if the noumena have no relationship to phenomena could they be unknowable. Kant, and his advocates in subsequent centuries, should have made some attempt to define noumena, using mathematical concepts, and should have derived testable predictions from their theoretical models. The only logical reason not to would be the dogmatic assertion that the noumena are beyond cognition; not just unknowable, but inconceivable as well.

Because Kant believed that a noumenal world beyond the empirical world must be unknowable, he attempted to re-define metaphysics. He believed that the faculties of cognition, the forms of experience, and the 'categories' of understanding exist independently of the content of our experience. Kant advocated the study of these things as metaphysics in the sense that they are independent of the content of experience. He urged that metaphysics should move away from speculation about the unknowable to study of the knowable. The false assumption in this reasoning is that a world beyond the empirical world must be unknowable.

Let us illustrate the claim that a metaphysical hypothesis should be formulated with the precise concepts of mathematics. One could hypothesize that both the transcendent, metaphysical world and the physical world are represented by mathematical structures, and they are related by a mathematical mapping. Let M denote the mathematical structure which represents the meta-physical world, and let N denote the mathematical structure which represents the physical world. One can postulate that both M and N must have

1. A cardinality

2. A topology

3. A dimension

4. A geometry

and one can postulate that they are related by a projection mapping M ! N which is

1. Non-injective, and therefore, non-invertible

2. Continuous
3. Either dimension-lowering or dimension-preserving

4. Non-isometric

Note that condition 2 relates to the topological notion of

continuity, and should not be confused with the cardinal notion of the continuum. A cardinality is not specified for either M or N . Even if both were discrete mathematical structures, they could each possess a topology, and the projection mapping could be continuous with respect to these topologies. Condition 3 means that the physical world, N , is either of lower dimension than the metaphysical world, M, or they are of equal dimension.

This particular metaphysical hypothesis is formally analogous to suggestions in some branches of physics that the universe has many more dimensions than we currently detect. For example, the original Kaluza-Klein theory predicted that the universe actually has 5 dimensions, and more recent versions predict many more dimensions. These theories have the empirically detectable 4-dimensional space-time diffeomorphically embedded in an n-dimensional manifold. The fields and geometry on the 4-dimensional submanifold are obtained from the n-dimensional manifold by what is either called a parallel or orthogonal projection. It must be conceded that these theories do not consider the n-dimensional reality to be metaphysical. In some cases, at least, this is because the n-dimensional reality is merely inaccessible at low-energies. Being detectable at higher energies, it is not a metaphysical reality. The fact that we cannot directly perceive the higher dimensions simply places them in the same category as the electron: they are empirically detectable, in principle, but not directly perceivable. The proposed relationship between the metaphysical world and the physical world is merely analogous to the relationship between the n-dimensional physical world and the perceptible world in Kaluza-Klein theories.

The relationship between the 3-dimensional physical world and phenomenal experience is also given by a projective transformation. The 3-dimensional physical world is projected onto the human retina, a 2-dimensional surface, by means of a perspective projection transformation. A perspective projection is simply a special case of the more general type of projective transformation which I defined above. The relationships between the 4-dimensional objects of general relativity and the measurements of an observer are also given by projection mappings.

To reiterate, the postulated projection mapping from the metaphysical world to the physical world is given to illustrate how a metaphysical hypothesis can be formulated with the precise concepts of mathematics. It is not intended to be a serious proposal. One can imagine other metaphysical hypotheses which do not satisfy this projective relationship. In fact, the computer program hypothesis might not satisfy this relationship. Notably, in the case of Platonic metaphysics, there appears to be a projective mapping in the opposite direction. If many objects in the physical world are instances of one Platonic form in the metaphysical 'Platonic realm', then there appears to be a projection mapping from the physical world to the Platonic realm.

Mathematics provides a vast resource of precise concepts which are just as applicable to metaphysics as they are to physics.3 Resistance to the application of mathematics in metaphysics could be founded on two possible objections:

• Mathematics is a non-foundational construction; the fundamental concepts one is trying to elucidate in metaphysics are taken for granted in mathematics; the fundamental concepts of mathematics are expressed in natural language. Hence, it might be argued, natural language is the appropriate medium for analysing foundational concepts.

• Mathematics is merely formal and abstract.

The first objection underestimates the capacity of mathematics to engage in foundational work. Mathematics is able to take the foundational concepts found in natural language, and generalise. For example, the Boolean logic expressed in natural language corresponds to the special case of a distributive lattice in a more general range of mathematical structures. The second objection fails to appreciate that the models of mathematical structures, i.e. the things which instantiate them, need not be constructed from numbers. Hence, the models of mathematical structures need not be abstract themselves. Physical objects can be the instances of mathematical structures, and so can metaphysical objects.

• Deriving empirical predictions from the metaphysical hypothesis

J.D.Barrow has claimed that if our universe is a computer program, then all the laws of physics must involve computable functions, (Barrow 1991, p205). A computable function is defined to be a function whose value can always be calculated by performing a finite sequence of well-defined steps, often called an 'effective procedure'. Certainly, if a universe unfolds in time on a computer, evolution equations must be used to calculate each time-step from the preceding time-step, and a solution of those evolution equations implemented on a computer must be a computable function. If the solutions of the fundamental evolution equations of physics were found to be non-computable functions, then the computer program hypothesis would be falsified. Whilst the computer program hypothesis therefore predicts that the solutions to the fundamental evo-lution equations of physics must be computable functions, computability would not be necessary to represent, at once, an entire space-time on a computer. Computability is only a requirement if the representation attempts to calculate one aspect of the universe from another aspect. As Tegmark remarks, "since we can choose to picture our Universe not as a 3D world where things happen, but as a 4D world that merely is, there is no need for the computer to compute anything at all - it could simply store all the 4D data," (Tegmark 1998, p26).

Note also that algorithmic compressibility is not a necessary condition to represent a universe on a computer. A digital representation of something is defined to be algorithmically compressible if the length, in bits, of the shortest program capable of generating that digital representation, is shorter than the length, in bits, of the digital representation itself. Our universe

285

might not be algorithmically compressible, but might still be digitally representable on a computer. What follows is an attempt to derive more specific empirical predictions from the computer program hypothesis.

To represent the entire universe on a computer one must use either:

• A unified theory of everything.

or

• A set of different theories, each with its own limited domain of applicability, such that the set of domains covers the entire universe.

We do not, at present, have a unified theory of everything, but we do have a set of different theories, which grow progressively closer to covering the entire universe, in all its detail. Of these, the only empirically verified theory which is capable of describing the universe as a whole is general relativity. However, although general relativity can represent the universe as a whole, when it does so, it is only concerned with the large scale structure of the universe. It cannot represent detail on all length scales, as a unified theory of everything could be expected to do. Nevertheless, because general relativity has been empirically verified, the predictions of a unified theory of everything would have to converge to the predictions of general relativity within general relativity's domain of applicability.

The physical predictions derived from the metaphysical computer program hypothesis will be derived from an examination of how to represent a general relativistic universe on a computer. This is perhaps a weak point of the strategy. The universe may not be a 4-dimensional Lorentzian manifold, as it is represented to be in general relativity. We do not know what type of thing a unified theory of everything, incorporating a theory of quantum gravity, would represent the universe to be. It is, therefore, a provisional decision to consider a universe created on a computer to be a general relativistic universe.

In addition, the predictions derived assume that a digital computer is the only type of computer which has the potential to simulate an entire universe. Although it isn't proven to be impossible for an analog computer to simulate an entire universe, the current evidence suggests that an analog computer cannot have the representational capacity to do so. An analog computer uses concrete (and continuous) physical quantities of one sort, (e.g. electrical quantities or hydraulic quantities), to represent concrete (and continuous) physical quantities of another sort, (e.g. the varying height of tides). In other words, an analog computer uses the concrete physical quantities of its physical components to represent the physical quantities of the system to be simulated. Early analog computers were constructed from levers, cogs, cams, discs and gears, and used mechanical motions to perform calculations. Modern analog computers tend to use electrical quantities, such as voltage levels, to represent the quantities of a simulated system, and specially designed circuits are used to perform arithmetic upon these voltage levels. Whilst an analog computer might use voltage levels to represent the values of quantities on a simulated system, a digital computer uses voltage levels to represent bits, and then sequences of bits encode the values of quantities on a simulated system. Analog computers tend to rely upon a mathematical resemblance between the pattern of quantity-values possessed by the machine and the pattern of quantity-values possessed by the simulated system.4 Analog computers do not use the versatile, encoded, abstract representation of physical quantities that a digital computer uses, and this limits their representational capacity.5

It is often claimed that the variables of an analog computer are, in fact, continuously variable, but this claim can be disputed. Variables such as electrical voltage or fluid pressure are probably discrete when they are reduced to the quantum level. Even if there are other variables which are genuinely continuous, it would still not be possible to precisely control their value. Suppose for the sake of argument that voltage is continuously variable. It would be impossible to set a precise input voltage of, say, 5:34V. The best one could ever do is to set an input voltage within some interval, say 5:34V § 0:01. This point is better illustrated for the case of irrational numbers. It is impossible to set an input voltage of ¼, and this is not because of the limitations of current technology, but because infinite precision is not attainable.

In general relativity, space is represented as a 3-dimensional differential manifold, and space-time is represented as a 4-dimensional differential manifold. A digital computer, as it is currently understood, can only deal with discrete items of data. The most crucial fact to recognize about a computer program is that the data objects defined in it are built from Z, the set of integers. In contrast, the objects of analytic mathematics are built from R, the set of real numbers. The memory of a classical, (i.e. non-quantum), digital computer consists of electronic circuits which have two possible voltage states. These voltage states are represented by binary digits, otherwise known as 'bits'. An element of memory is therefore called a 'bit'. Each bit of memory has two possible states, represented as 0 and 1. The set of possible states of a bit can be represented as $Z2 = Z=2Z$ = f0; 1g, the additive group of integers, modulo 2. Z2 is a realisation of the cyclic group of two elements. Each byte of memory, a string of 8 bits, and the smallest addressable unit of memory, can be represented by

$$(Z2)8 = Z2 \text{ £ } Z2 \text{ £ } Z2 \text{ £ } Z2 \text{ £ } Z2 \text{ £ } Z2 \text{ £ } Z2 \text{ £ } Z2;$$

the 8-fold Cartesian product of Z2. Thus, for a classical computer with n bytes of memory, the entire memory can be represented by (Z2)8n, a discrete mathematical structure of 8n dimensions. All the data objects defined in a program correspond to regions of memory, hence the data objects defined in a program are built from subsets of the discrete mathematical structure (Z2)8n.

The memory of a quantum computer consists of physical systems which possess a quantum state space isomorphic to the 2-dimensional complex Hilbert space C2. Each such memory element is referred to as a 'qubit', or 'Qbit'. A string of n qubits is represented by the n-fold tensor product of C2. Hence, the state of 8 qubits is represented by a vector in

(C2)8 = C2 - C2 - C2 - C2 - C2 - C2 - C2 - C2

As a consequence, the state of the n qubits can be quantum mechanically en-tangled.

Each qubit is considered to have a fixed basis, fv0; v1g. Each vector in the n-fold tensor product consists of a complex linear combination of the 2n basis

vectors fvi1 - ¢ ¢ ¢ - vin : i1 = 0; 1; :::; in = 0; 1g. The algorithms of a quantum computer correspond to unitary operators upon these complex Hilbert spaces.

Because C2 is built from the set of real numbers, and because each qubit C2 possesses a continuum of quantum states, it might appear that a quantum computer can store an infinite amount of information. This appearance, however, is deceptive. Whilst there are a continuum of possible unitary operators on a qubit Hilbert space, each quantum computer will only be engineered to implement a finite collection. Moreover, each quantum computation must cease with a measurement of the state of the n qubits, and this collapses the state from a linear combination of the basis vectors into one of the fixed basis vectors, vi1 - ¢ ¢ ¢ - vin . The initial state on which the unitary transformations can operate is also such a state, and as Mermin comments, "the entire role of the state of the Qbits at any stage of a succession of unitary transformations is to encapsulate the probability of the outcomes, should the final measurement be made at that stage of the process," (2002, p16). Thus, a quantum computer, like a classical computer, possesses a finite number of accessible states. In fact, n qubits of memory possess exactly the same number of accessible states as n bits of memory, namely 2n. The data objects defined in a program running on a quantum computer are discrete objects.

Because every manifold has the cardinality of the continuum, and because digital computers can only represent discrete objects, it is impossible to exactly represent a manifold on a digital computer. It is, therefore, impossible on a digital computer to exactly represent space and space-time as they are represented in general relativity.

If space and space-time actually are manifolds, and if a manifold cannot be exactly represented on a digital computer, then space and space-time cannot be exactly represented on a digital computer. If the space and space-time of our universe cannot be exactly represented on a digital computer, then our universe cannot be a computer program running on a digital computer in another universe.

However, as already mentioned, the space and space-time of our universe may not actually be manifolds. Space and space-time may not exactly be as they are represented to be in general relativity. Perhaps space and space-time are discrete, and perhaps the manifolds of general relativity only provide an idealisation of a discrete reality. The space and space-time of our universe can only be exactly represented on a computer if space and space-time are discrete.

Loop quantum gravity offers, perhaps, a mathematically rigorous means to quantize general relativity, and loop quantum gravity suggests that space is discrete in some sense. Using Ashtekar's 'new variables' approach, canonical general relativity can be cast in the form of a canonical gauge theory, albeit a gauge theory with additional constraints to the Gauss constraint. The configuration space is a space of SU(2)-connections on a principal fibre bundle over a 3-manifold Σ. In loop quantum gravity, each closed curve ('loop') in the

3-manifold defines a functional on the space of SU(2)-connections. This functional is obtained by taking the holonomy of each connection around the loop, representing that group element as an operator on a vector space, and then taking the trace of that operator. Furthermore, each 'spin network' embedded in the 3-manifold defines a functional on the space of SU(2)-connections. A spin network, treated in isolation, is a discrete mathematical object consisting of a graph, (a collection of vertices and edges), an irreducible representation of SU(2) assigned to each edge, and an 'intertwining' operator between such representations assigned to each vertex. Such a graph embedded in the 3-manifold Σ defines a functional on the space of SU(2)-connections by taking the holonomy of a connection along each edge, using the representations to obtain operators along each edge, forming the tensor product of all those operators, tensoring that with all the intertwining operators, and then contracting to obtain a number, the number assigned to the connection, (Baez 1995, p19). Such functionals turn out to be eigenvectors of operators which purportedly represent the area of surfaces in the 3-manifold and the volume of regions in the 3-manifold. Furthermore, these operators have discrete spectra.

If one accepts that quantum theory provides a complete description of a physical system, then, arguably, it is not the configurations of the classical system which exist, but the quantum state function(al). Hence, in the case of loop quantum gravity, the 3-manifold used to define the classical configuration space does not exist. Rather, it is the state functional defined by the spin network which exists.

Many important questions remain. For example, the dynamics of loop quantum gravity remain intransigent, and there is no obvious classical limit to the theory. Whilst it is claimed that area and volume are discrete, what are they the area and volume of, if a 3-manifold does not exist? Are area and volume re-interpreted as properties of spin networks?

The established means of finding a discrete approximation to a manifold, is to find a cell complex which is homeomorphic to the manifold. In particular, one tries to find a simplicial complex which is homeomorphic to the manifold. The schema of the simplicial complex is a discrete mathematical object, which can be exactly represented on a computer. By representing the schema on a computer, one approximately represents the manifold.

If the schema of a simplicial complex is the natural discrete approximation to a manifold, then, conversely, the manifold can be said to be the natural continuum idealisation of the schema. If space and space-time are actually discrete, but if they can also be represented in a continuum idealisation as a 3-manifold and 4-manifold, respectively, then it is natural to suggest that space is actually a 3-dimensional schema, and space-time is actually a 4-dimensional schema. Regge calculus is generally considered to be the 'discretized' version of general relativity, and Regge calculus duly represents space and space-time as a simplicial complex.

Loop quantum gravity demonstrates that, although space and space-time might not be manifolds, they might not be the schema of simplicial complexes either. However, if space and space-time actually are discrete, it may be that they are best represented by loop quantum gravity on small scales, and best represented by the schema of simplicial complexes on large scales.

Some explanation of the mathematics is in order here. An n-cell is an object which is homeomorphic with the n-ball in n-dimensional Euclidean space, $D_n = \{x \in R_n : \|x\| = 1\}$. For example, a 2-ball is a disc, bounded by a circle, while a 3-ball is a solid ball bounded by a 2-sphere. Any polygon is homeomorphic with a 2-ball, and is therefore a 2-cell. Any solid polyhedron is homeomorphic with a 3-ball, and is therefore a 3-cell.

A cell-complex is obtained by pasting together any number of cells, so that the faces of the cells are either disjoint, or so that they coincide completely. A 3-dimensional cell-complex is obtained by pasting together 3-cells in such a way that the faces, edges and vertices of the cells are either disjoint, or they coincide completely.

The most interesting type of cell is a simplex. A 0-simplex is a point, or 'vertex', a 1-simplex is a line segment, or 'edge', a 2-simplex is a triangle, and a 3-simplex is a solid tetrahedron. By pasting together simplices, one obtains a simplicial complex, (see Stillwell 1992, p23-24). A 3-dimensional simplicial complex is obtained by pasting together solid tetrahedra. The schema of a 3-dimensional simplicial complex can be specified as follows. First, one declares all the vertices in the complex. Next, one can specify which subsets of the set of vertices correspond to simplexes. By specifying a pair of vertices, fPi; Pjg, one indicates that those vertices are connected by an edge. One can then specify which triples fPi; Pj; Pkg of vertices correspond to the faces, and finally one can list which quadruples fPi; Pj; Pk; Plg of vertices correspond to the tetrahedra. One could alternatively give each edge a name, and then specify which triples of adjoining edges are connected by a face. One would then name each face, and specify which quadruples of adjoining faces are connected by a tetrahedron, (see Geroch and Hartle 1986, p546).

Although the manifold models of general relativity may be idealisations, one particular manifold model may eventually be verified by observation, to the exclusion of all others. To be specific, either a Friedmann-Roberston-Walker (FRW) model, a small perturbation of a FRW model, or an exact solution close to a FRW model, may be verified by astronomical observation. If the computer program hypothesis predicts that space or space-time is actually the schema of a simplicial complex on large scales, then the manifold model of the large-scale universe must be homeomorphic with a simplicial complex whose schema can be represented on a computer. It is therefore important to determine which manifold models of general relativity can be discretely represented on a digital computer by the schema of a simplicial complex. If a particular manifold model were to be verified by

298

astronomical observation, but that model could not be represented by a schema on a digital computer, then the hypothesis that our universe is a computer program running on a digital computer would be falsified.

Suppose, then, that one tries to represent space-time on a computer with the schema of a 4-dimensional simplicial complex. Unfortunately, it is not known if every 4-manifold is homeomorphic to a simplicial complex. Hence, there may be 4-manifolds which cannot be discretely represented by the schema of a simplicial complex. If the space-time of the universe has a manifold idealisation which does not have a homeomorphic simplicial complex, then the space-time of the universe would not be representable on a computer by the schema of a simplicial complex. If there were no other means of discretely representing such a 4-manifold on a computer, then the space-time of the universe would not be representable on a digital computer.

More seriously, because a computer can only store a finite amount of data, it can only represent the schema of a finite simplicial complex, a simplicial complex which contains a finite number of simplexes. A finite simplicial complex can only be homeomorphic to a compact manifold, hence only a compact 4-manifold is discretely representable by a schema on a computer. Unfortunately, a compact 4-manifold cannot accept a Lorentzian metric. If the space-time of our universe is Lorentzian, then our universe can only be a non-compact Lorentzian 4-manifold. One possible conclusion to draw is that one cannot represent a universe like our own on a computer if one tries to represent the entire 4-dimensional history of the universe.

As an alternative, the geometrodynamical formulation of general relativity employs a so-called '3+1' decomposition of space-time. One chooses a 3-manifold Σ, and one studies the time-evolution of the geometry and matter fields on Σ. As the geometry and matter fields evolve, a 4-dimensional space-time unfolds. Such a space-time will, of necessity, have the topology of R1 £ Σ. The geometrodynamics formulation is advantageous because of Moise's triangulation theorem for 3-manifolds, (Stillwell 1992, p25 and p242). Moise demonstrated that every 3-manifold is homeomorphic with a simplicial complex; one says that every 3-manifold can be 'triangulated'. Although it is true that every n-manifold can be triangulated for n · 3, it is, to reiterate, unknown whether all 4-manifolds can be triangulated.

Moise's theorem means that any possible topology of the

spatial universe can be discretely represented with the schema of a 3-dimensional simplicial complex. Once again, however, a digital computer can only represent the schema of a finite simplicial complex. Whilst a compact 3-manifold is homeomorphic with a finite simplicial complex, a non-compact 3-manifold can only be homeomorphic with an infinite simplicial complex, a complex which contains an infinite number of simplexes.

Only a compact 3-manifold can be homeomorphic with a 3-dimensional simplicial complex whose schema is representable on a digital computer. Hence, if our universe is a program running on a digital computer, then our spatial uni-verse must have a compact spatial topology in a continuum idealisation. The hypothesis that our universe is a program on a digital computer, predicts that the spatial universe is discrete, and yields the potentially testable prediction that our universe has compact spatial topology in a continuum idealisation.

The prediction of compact spatial topology means that the Euclidean R3 and hyperbolic H3 FRW universes are both inconsistent with the computer program hypothesis. The only FRW universe which has both simply connected and compact spatial topology, is the S3-universe. Hence, the only simply connected FRW universe which could be discretely represented on a computer, is the S3-universe. There are, however, a host of multiply connected compact FRW universes. The spatial geometry of each such universe is obtained as a quotient $\Sigma=$ of a simply connected Riemannian space form6 Σ, where is a discrete, properly discontinuous, fixed-point free subgroup of the isometry group $I(\Sigma)$, (O'Neill 1983, p243 and Boothby 1986, p406, Theorem 6.5).

Compact FRW models exist for any value of sectional curvature k. Of the 18 flat, k = 0, 3-dimensional Riemannian space forms, 10 are compact. Given that one can only create compact FRW universes on a computer, it follows that one can only create 10 topologically different k = 0 FRW universes on a computer.

All of the 3-dimensional Riemannian space forms of constant positive curvature are compact, hence they could all be created on a computer.

Whilst there are compact and non-compact quotients H3= , there are an infinite number of such compact quotients. The work of Thurston demonstrates that 'most' compact and orientable 3-manifolds can be equipped with a complete Riemannian metric tensor of constant negative sectional curvature. This means that 'most' compact, orientable 3-manifolds can be obtained as a quotient H3= of hyperbolic 3-space.7 One can therefore create an infinite number of possible negative curvature FRW universes on a computer. However, there is no compact k = ¡1 space form which is globally homogeneous. H3 itself is the only globally homogeneous 3-dimensional Riemannian space form of constant negative curvature, and H3 is, of course, non-compact. Given that one can only create a compact universe on a computer, one cannot create a k = ¡1 FRW universe on a computer which is globally homogeneous. Thus, if our own universe is a globally homogeneous k = ¡1 FRW universe, it cannot exist on a computer. However, a locally homogeneous k = ¡1 FRW universe, with compact, multiply connected topology, could exist on a computer, and it is only local homogeneity which our astronomical observations are capable of detecting.

In practice it is difficult to test the prediction of compact spatial topology. Observational evidence currently indicates that our universe is a FRW universe, but there is no observable parameter in a FRW model which determines the spatial topology. Thus, there is no necessary link between the spatial topology of a FRW universe and the value of the density parameter $\Omega 0$; one cannot infer the spatial topology of our universe from $\Omega 0$.

However, in a 'small', compact, multiply connected universe, it is possible to see around the entire universe. To understand this, begin by recalling that a Riemannian manifold $(\Sigma; °)$ has a natural metric space structure. The metric tensor $°$ determines a Riemannian distance $d(p; q)$ between any pair of points $p; q \in \Sigma$. The Riemannian distance $d(p; q)$ is dimensionless, in the sense that it lacks any physical units. In a FRW model, it is the scale factor $R(t)$ which introduces physical units of distance. The physical distance between p and q at time t is $R(t)d(p; q)$. Because $R(t)$ has physical units, so does $R(t)d(p; q)$.

For any FRW universe, one can calculate the maximum Riemannian distance, dmax, that light has travelled by a time t0, which is considered to be the present time. The relevant equation is
$$Z t0 \quad c$$

$$dmax(t0) = 0 \quad R(t) \, dt$$

A civilization located at some point p in space, will, at time t0, be able to see no further, in any direction, than a Riemannian distance of dmax(t0). This distance can therefore be referred to as the Riemannian horizon distance. It is, of course, a dimensionless quantity.

Now, recalling that the diameter of a metric space is the supremum of the distances which can separate pairs of points, it is a fact that any compact Riemannian manifold is a metric space of finite diameter. If one created, on a computer, a FRW universe in which $(\Sigma; °)$ were a compact Riemannian manifold of sufficiently small diameter, diam $(\Sigma; °)$, then the Riemannian horizon

distance dmax(t0) could exceed diam $(\Sigma; °)$ by the time t0 » 1010. If so, the horizon would have disappeared for the observers in that universe. They would

be able to see their entire spatial universe. No point of their universe could be separated from them by a Riemannian distance greater than diam $(\Sigma; °)$, so if dmax(t0) ˌ diam $(\Sigma; °)$, then they would be able to receive light from all regions of their spatial universe.

In such universes, individual galaxies and clusters of galaxies would produce multiple images upon the celestial sphere of planet-bound observers, (see Ellis 1971). Different compact spatial topologies and geometries would produce different patterns of ghost

305

images and multiple images upon the celestial sphere.

However, although compact spatial topology is a necessary condition for the entire spatial universe to be visible, it is not a sufficient condition. Our universe might have compact spatial topology, but if it is a 'large' compact universe, then all of space will not be visible. For all of space to be visible when the universe is only » 1010 yrs old, the Riemannian manifold $(\Sigma; °)$ which represents the spatial universe must be sufficiently small, as well as compact, Even if our spatial universe is small and compact, it would be extremely difficult to identify multiple images of galaxy clusters. Hence, although the presence of multiple images would verify the hypothesis of a small, compact universe, the fact that they have not been identified at the current time does not falsify the hypothesis. A better means of testing the hypothesis is to search for paired circles in the microwave background radiation. Recent research indicates that if such paired circles exist, then one could derive the spatial topology from the specific pattern of paired circles, (see Cornish, Spergel, Starkman 1998). The CMBR power spectrum can also be used to determine whether our spatial universe is a small compact universe. A small compact universe would affect the CMBR power spectrum on large angular scales. The WMAP satellite has revealed anomalies in the CMBR power spectrum on large angular scales. The quadrupole $l = 2$ mode was found to be about 1=7 the strength predicted for an infinite flat universe, while the octopole $l = 3$ mode was 72% of the strength predicted for such a non-compact $k = 0$ universe, (Luminet et al 2003, p3).

The presence of paired circles or specific anomalies in the CMBR power spectrum would verify that the universe is spatially compact, and would thereby verify the computer program hypothesis. Unfortunately, the absence of paired circles or anomalies in the power spectrum would not entail that the spatial universe is non-compact. Our universe could simply be a large compact universe. Hence, the absence of paired circles or anomalies in the power spectrum would not falsify the computer program hypothesis.

Predictions about the lifetime of our universe are easier to test than predictions about the spatial topology. The lifetime of our universe is determined by parameters such as the Hubble parameter H0 and the density parameter $\Omega 0$, which can be inferred from observation. Hence, if the computer program hypothesis made predictions about the lifetime of our universe, it would be easier to test it. If a universe is represented by a

Lorentzian manifold (M; g), then the lifetime of the universe corresponds to the 'timelike diameter' of (M; g). The timelike diameter of (M; g) is the supremum of the length of all past-directed timelike curves in (M; g). As Beem and Ehrlich comment, "the timelike diameter represents the supremum of possible proper times any particle could possibly experience in the given space-time," (Beam and Ehrlich 1980, p329).

If a Lorentzian manifold with an infinite timelike diameter were represented by a numerical solution of the Einstein geometrodynamics equations, and if the size of the time steps in the numerical solution were constant, then an infinite number of time steps would be necessary. An infinite amount of information would have to be processed. Alternatively, if the size of the time steps diverge exponentially as t ! 1, a numerical solution would only require a finite number of time steps. The ever-expanding k · 0 FRW universes are examples of universes with an infinite lifetime. If a computer in a universe with an infinite lifetime could process information at a constant rate, then it could process an infinite amount of information. However, an ever-expanding universe will suffer an entropy 'heat death', the amount of free energy available converging to zero as t ! 1. Brillouin's inequality entails that there is a minimum, positive amount of free energy which must be expended to process a bit of information. Where I is the amount of information processed in bits,

I ·   E=kBT ln 2

Not only could the computer program hypothesis be falsified by empirical investigation, but there are logical constraints upon what it is possible to simulate on a computer.

A computer is a finite volume subsystem of a universe which is capable of representing the state of other systems. A system can represent, exactly and completely, the state of another system, if and only if the amount of information which can be coded in the first system is greater than or equal to the amount of information which can be coded in the other system. An entire universe is a special type of system. Hence, a subsystem of a universe A can represent, exactly and completely, the state of a universe B, if and only if the amount of information which can be coded in the subsystem of A is greater than or equal to the amount of information which can be coded in universe B.

As a special case, if the amount of information which can be coded in a subsystem of a universe A is less than the amount of information which can be coded in the entire universe A , then it is impossible for the subsystem of universe A to represent, exactly and completely, the entire universe A .

The amount of information which can be coded in a system is determined by the number of possible different states of the system. If N denotes the number of possible states, then the amount of information I which can be coded, in bits, is simply I = log2N. Hence, if the number of possible states of a subsystem of a universe is less than the number of possible states of the entire universe, then it is impossible for that subsystem to represent, exactly and completely, the entire universe.

However, just because a system is a subsystem of a universe, it does not follow that the number of possible states of the system is less than the number of possible states of the universe. True, if the number of possible states of a subsystem is finite, then by virtue of being a subsystem, that finite number must be smaller than the number of possible states of the entire universe. For every state of a subsystem, there must be multiple states of the entire universe which induce the same state upon that subsystem, hence the number of possible states of the entire universe must be larger. However, if the number of possible states of a subsystem is not finite, then it is possible that it has the same number of possible states as the entire universe. A priori, it is quite possible that a subsystem of a universe A , and the entire universe A , both possess an infinite number of states. If the state space of a subsystem has the same cardinality as the state space of the entire universe, then, by definition, there exists at least one bijective mapping between the two state spaces. Any such bijective mapping would enable the states of the entire universe to be represented by the states of the subsystem.

This argument can be presented in another way. If a subsystem S of our universe represents the entire universe U , it must also represent S representing U . If it does this, it must also represent S representing S representing U . And so on, ad infinitum. This is possible only if the subsystem can store an infinite amount of information.

If the entire universe only has a finite number of possible states, then a subsystem will also have a finite number of states, and the number of subsystem states will be smaller than the number of universe states. However, if the entire universe has an infinite number of possible states, then a subsystem could have either a finite number or an infinite number of possible states.

If the entire universe has an infinite number of possible states, then it could conceivably possess either a continuous infinity of possible states, or a discrete infinity. A digital computer could only represent the universe exactly if the universe is discrete, hence the only case of interest is the case in which the universe has a discrete infinity of possible states. A digital computer could only represent the universe exactly and completely if the entire universe and the computer subsystem of the universe both possess a discrete infinity of possible states. In other words, a digital computer could only represent the universe exactly and completely if both the computer and the universe can code a discrete infinity of information.

A computer is a finite volume subsystem of the universe, hence to determine if a computer could code the same amount of information as the entire universe, it is necessary to determine if a finite volume subsystem can code a finite or infinite amount of information. To answer this question, it is necessary to determine what the physical structure of the universe is.

At present, it appears that there are discrete levels of

physical structure in the universe. All macroscopic material objects in our universe are composed of chemical elements and chemical compounds. The latter are composed of atoms in different combinations and organizations. Atoms are composed of electrons and atomic nuclei. The nuclei of atoms are themselves composed of protons and neutrons, which are themselves composed of quarks. The parts of material objects do not appear to lie on a continuum.

Electrons and quarks are purported to be elementary particles, pieces of matter which have no parts. If elementary particles do exist, then our universe could be said to have a finite lower level of structure. There would be no levels of structure below the level of elementary particles.

I propose that a finite volume subsystem is limited to coding a finite amount of information if and only if the following three conditions are satisfied:

The number of structure levels available in a finite volume of space is finite.

• On each structure level, there is a finite set of parts in a finite volume of space.

- Each of the parts on each level of structure has a finite set of states.

A finite volume subsystem which satisfies these conditions has only a finite number of possible states, and therefore cannot code the same amount of information which can be coded in the entire universe.

To reiterate, a computer could only represent the universe exactly and completely if a finite volume subsystem can code a discrete infinity of information. It seems safe to assume that, on each level of structure, there is a finite set of parts in any finite volume of space. The Bekenstein bound and the so-called holographic bound of Susskind and 't Hooft, purportedly entail that the parts on each level of structure have a finite set of states, (Bekenstein 2003). More-over, the existence of elementary particles would mean that there is a finite set of structure levels in each finite volume of space. It would appear, therefore, at first sight, that all three conditions are satisfied. It would appear that a finite volume subsystem cannot code a discrete infinity of information, and it would appear that a computer cannot represent the universe exactly and completely.

However, further thought raises some doubts. Both the Bekenstein bound and the holographic bound place an upper limit on the entropy within a finite volume of space. Given a finite quantity of weakly self-gravitating energy E in a spherical volume of radius R, which is isolated from other systems, (Bekenstein 2004), the entropy S is subject to the following upper bound:

$$S \cdot 2\frac{1}{4}ER =^\sim c :$$

The holographic bound is independent of the quantity of energy, and places the following limit on the entropy of a spherical volume of radius R, which is isolated from other systems:

$$S \cdot \frac{1}{4}c3R2 =^\sim G :$$

In both cases, it is then assumed that a finite upper limit to the entropy of a finite volume of space entails a finite upper limit to the information storage capacity of that volume. This might be inferred from the following relationship:

Information = Maximum entropy ¡ entropy :

By implication, it is the statistical states or macrostates of a system which are the bearers of entropy and information here. The states which provide a complete, detailed description of a system are referred to as 'microstates'. A statistical state expresses only partial knowledge of the state of a system, and, in classical mechanics at least, corresponds to a probability distribution ½ defined upon the space of microstates . A macrostate is a set of macroscopically indistinguishable microstates M , and corresponds to a special type of statistical state in which the probability distribution is of a constant value j M j¡1 on M , and zero elsewhere. j M j denotes the volume of M . The microstate of a system inherits the entropy and information of the macrostate to which it belongs. The entropy of an isolated system increases because the microstate of the system moves into macrostates of ever greater entropy. The equation above means that the information possessed by a system at a point in time is the difference between the maximum entropy of the system, and the entropy possessed by the system at that point in time. The maximum information which can be possessed by a system is that which it possesses when the system's entropy is zero. Hence, according to the relationship above, the maximum information equals the maximum entropy.

Whether this entails that a finite volume of space possesses a finite number of states is a different question. In classical mechanics, a system consisting of n particles has a 6n-dimensional continuum state space , called the phase space. The entropy $S(\frac{1}{2})$ of statistical state $\frac{1}{2}$ in classical mechanics is defined to be

$$S(\frac{1}{2}) = ¡kB \quad \overset{Z}{} \quad \frac{1}{2} \log \frac{1}{2} \, d^1 ;$$

where kB is Boltzmann's constant. In the case of a macrostate $\frac{1}{2}M$, this reduces to

$$S(\frac{1}{2}M) = ¡kB \, Z \, M \, j \, M \, j¡1 \log j \, M \, j¡1 d^1$$
$$= ¡kB \, j \, M \, j¡1$$
$$\overset{Z}{}$$
$$\log 1 \, ¡ \log j \, M \, j d^1$$
$$\overset{Z}{}$$

$$\overset{M}{} = kB \, j \, M \, j¡1 \quad \log j \, M \, j d^1$$
$$\overset{M}{}$$

$$= kB \log j \, M \, j :$$

Hence, although the entropy of a macrostate of such a

system can be fi-nite, it corresponds to a continuum of possible microstates. An upper limit to entropy does not entail a finite number of possible states. I propose that the link between entropy and information storage capacity is only valid for finite state-space systems. When a system has an infinite number of states, but a finite maximum entropy, I propose that it has an infinite information storage capacity. Ultimately, each different state of a system can represent different information, so a system with an infinite number of possible states, but a finite volume state space, and therefore a finite maximum entropy, nevertheless has an infinite information storage capacity.

To argue that a finite volume of space possesses a finite information storage capacity, one might alternatively start from loop quantum gravity, and try to argue that a finite volume of space only possesses a finite number of quantum states. A finite volume of space corresponds to a finite number of spin network nodes, and for a fixed finite number of nodes, there are a finite number of spin network states. For a system with a finite number of microstates, each macrostate M corresponds to an equivalence class containing a finite number of microstates, Num(M). The entropy of such a macrostate is simply

$S = k_B \log \text{Num}(M)$:

Hence, a system with a finite number of microstates possesses a finite maximum entropy, and therefore possesses an upper limit on its information storage capacity.

However, quantum theory may not be the definitive theory of the physical world. A quantum state may correspond to many, or an infinite number of actual states. Even though there may be only a finite number of quantum states for a finite volume of space, there may be an infinite number of actual states. It may be that quantum theory is only valid for certain levels of structure, and it might merely be that the amount of information which can be coded above a certain length scale, or the amount of information which can be coded in a certain way, is finite.

There is also no decisive evidence that elementary particles exist. If the current candidates for elementary particles, such as quarks, do have parts, then those parts might only be detectable at energies which are not currently available in particle accelerators.

One could also dispute the assumption that, on each level of structure, there is a finite set of parts in any finite volume of space. If each part has a non-zero spatial extension with a well-defined boundary, and if the parts cannot inter-penetrate, then it does indeed follow that there can only be a finite set of parts packed into a finite volume of space. However, parts in quantum theory do seem able to interpenetrate each other to some degree. If there are levels of structure below the levels of the electron and quark, one might find very strange things, beyond even quantum theory, like an infinite number of parts interpenetrating each other in a finite volume of space.

Tipler claims that there could be a hierarchy of computer universes, just like the hierarchy of so-called 'virtual machines' which can exist on a computer, and he claims that we would not know which level of the hierarchy our own universe exists at. Whilst I have argued that the Bekenstein bound does not entail that a finite volume subsystem has only a finite number of possible states, Tipler accepts this implication. This, I propose, is inconsistent with the claim that we would not know which level of a universe hierarchy our own universe exists at.

When one computer is programmed so that it precisely mimics the input-output behaviour of another computer, the latter is said to be emulated by the former. The emulation program, running on the real computer, is said to be a virtual machine. A real machine T1 can be programmed to emulate another, producing a virtual machine T2. The virtual machine T2 can then be programmed to emulate another computer, producing a higher level virtual machine T3. These levels are referred to as levels of implementation.

A universe running on a computer could itself contain computers, upon which other universes are running. The universes would be running at different levels of implementation, and Tipler suggests, (1995, p208), that in this case, the levels should be thought of as levels of reality. Tipler seems to assume that there must be a lowest level of the hierarchy, and refers to this as 'ultimate reality'. Tipler claims that "we cannot know if the universe in which we find ourselves is actually ultimate reality," (ibid.).

However, whilst any one computer may be able to emulate the input-output behaviour of another, that does not entail that any one computer has the same representational capacity as another. An actual computer, with a finite memory, does not have the same representational capacity as every other computer. A computer with N bytes of memory does not have the same representational capacity as a computer with M bytes of memory if M > N. There may be data structures which the computer with M bytes of memory can represent, but which the computer with N bytes cannot.

It was argued above that a computer with a finite set of states, (and hence a finite memory), cannot perfectly represent the universe to which it belongs. This is because a computer with a finite memory cannot code the same amount of information as the universe to which it belongs. In general, a computer with a finite memory cannot perfectly represent any universe which can code a greater amount of information than the computer. Any universe which can code a greater amount of information than the universe to which the computer belongs, will code more information than the computer.

If one accepts Tipler's claim that "complexity is appropriately measured by the number of possible alternative states a system can be in," (1995, p118), then the complexity of a system can also be measured as the amount of information which that system can code.9 If one accepts that a finite volume subsystem has only a finite number of possible states, then a computer can only have a finite memory. If a computer can only have a finite memory, then a computer cannot perfectly represent a universe of the same complexity, or greater complexity, than the universe to which the computer belongs. The complexity of a universe is observable, hence, contra Tipler, the levels of implementation are distinguishable. If a finite volume subsystem has only a finite number of possible states, then each higher level of universe implementation is less complex than the level below. A computer with a finite memory cannot perfectly represent a universe unless that universe is simpler than the universe to which the computer belongs. The more complex the universe one belongs to, the lower down the hierarchy that universe is placed. A universe of maximal complexity, if there is such a thing, could be proven to be the universe of ultimate reality.

If our universe is a computer program running on a computer in another universe, then that universe must have a higher level of complexity to our own. This greater complexity might take the form of a higher number of spatial dimensions. If the metaphysical universe has a higher number of dimensions than our own, this would be consistent with the proposal for a projective relationship between a metaphysical reality and a physical reality.

Of course, if a finite volume subsystem has a discrete infinity of possible states, then a computer might be able to perfectly represent a universe with the same complexity as the universe to which the computer belongs. If so, then the levels of universe implementation might all have the same level of complexity. The point is that, if the Bekenstein bound does entail that a finite volume subsystem has only a finite number of possible states, then the Bekenstein bound is inconsistent with the thesis that universes at different levels of implementation are indistinguishable.

• Reductionism, identity, and universe creation on a computer

The suggestion that a physical system can be perfectly simulated on a computer appears to have antireductionistic implications. Suppose, for example, that a tornado could be perfectly simulated on a computer. A tornado is described by a solution of the Navier-Stokes equations.10 To simulate a tornado on a computer, one would define program variables to represent the air pressure, velocity, density etc. in a volume of space, and one would represent the tornado by calculating a solution of the Navier-Stokes equations for these variables. Whilst a 'real' tornado is realised

324

upon a collection of air molecules, a simulated tornado is realised upon the components and circuitry of a computer. Hence, if a tornado could be perfectly simulated on a computer, then a tornado could be realised on more than one medium. Two completely different lower-level processes would correspond to the same higher-level process.

Epistemological reductionism asserts that what can be known or theoretically represented about the higher levels of a composite system can be reduced to what can be known or theoretically represented about the lower levels. Ontological reductionism asserts that what exists on the higher levels of a composite system can be reduced to what exists on the lower levels. I propose that ontological reductionism is the conjunction of the two following assertions:

1. The higher-level properties of a composite system uniquely determine the parts of the system and the way in which the parts are organized and interact. In other words, the higher-level properties of a composite system uniquely determine the properties of the subsystems and the relationships between the subsystems.

2. The parts of a system, and the way in which the

parts are organized and interact, uniquely determine the higher-level properties of the system. In other words, the properties of the subsystems in a composite system, and the relationships between the subsystems, uniquely determines the higher-level properties of the composite system.

The second assertion on its own is ontological supervenience. This is the idea that there can be no difference in the higher-level state of a composite system without a difference in the lower-level state, otherwise one would have a one-many correspondence between the lower-level states and higher-level states.

Some of the expressions used here require some explanation. A composite system is simply a system composed of multiple parts, whilst a higher-level property of a composite system is a property which can be possessed by the whole system. In some cases, such as shape and size, a higher-level property can also be possessed by the subsystems. In other cases, a higher-level property cannot be possessed by any individual part. For example, liquidity is a higher-level property of matter which can only be possessed by a collection of particles. Liquidity cannot be possessed by an individual particle.

326

If a system satisfies some law of physics, then that law of physics is a property of the system. If the system is a composite system, and it satisfies some law of physics, then that law of physics is a higher-level property of the system. In one sense, the laws of physics are properties of properties of physical systems, or relationships between the properties of a physical system. If energy, position, and velocity, for example, are properties of physical systems, then evolution equations govern the time evolution of these properties, and constraint equations govern the possible relationships between the different properties.

The claim that the laws of Nature are relationships among properties is part of the 'N-relation' account of the laws of Nature. Consider the example

• = M a. There are two levels on which this law expresses a relationship between properties. The first level relationship is between the general properties of acceleration, force and mass. This is a relationship between so-called 'determinable' properties. This relationship between determinable properties entails an infinite number of other relationships between the so-called 'determinates' of those properties.

Determinates are more specific properties: If the property of mass is a determinable property, then a mass of 3:0 kg, or a mass of 23:7kg, are examples of determinate properties. The general relationship $F = M a$ entails an infinite number of relationships between the determinates. For example, an acceleration of 5ms¡2, a mass of 10kg, and a force of 50N, are so related. How-ever, even a determinate property such as a mass of 3:0 kg, is a universal, which can be possessed by different objects at different times and places. One can have many different instances of a mass of 3:0 kg. Hence, on a third level, the general law expresses a relationship between all instances of the determinants

.The organization and interaction between the parts of a composite system includes both the spatial arrangement of the parts, and the mutual forces exerted between them. For example, if the parts are atoms or molecules, the properties of the composite system depend upon whether the parts are arranged randomly or as a crystal lattice, and depend upon whether the electromagnetic bonds between the parts are covalent bonds, or Van de Waals bonds, etc.

Statement 1 claims that the entire set of higher-level properties, in combination, determines uniquely the parts of the system and the way they are organized and interact. Individual higher-level properties can be possessed by many different systems, composed of different parts. For example, liquidity is a higher-level property which can be possessed by many different chemical substances. Liquidity is not a property unique to water. A collection of helium atoms, or mercury atoms, for example, can be in a liquid state. Hence, liquidity is a higher-level property of a system which does not uniquely determine the parts of the system. The parts of any liquid body do interact in a similar manner, whatever the types of particle involved, hence liquidity, as a higher-level property, does determine the type of the relationships between the parts, but it does not determine what the parts will be. Furthermore, the specific liquid properties, such as viscosity, density, or pressure, will be different for different chemicals. Liquids of different chemical composition will all share the property of liquidity, but they will differ in the complete range of higher-level properties they possess.

If a physical system could be realised on more than one medium, this would entail the falsity of statement 1. It would not, however, affect statement 2, the principle of supervenience. For example, the properties of a tornado might not determine a unique medium upon which it must be realised, but the properties of air molecules, and the relationships between air molecules entail that a tornado can be realised on a collection of air molecules. Similarly, if it were possible to realise a tornado on a computer, then it would be the properties of, and relationships between, the components and circuitry of a computer which would entail that a tornado can be realised upon a computer.

Whether or not a physical system can in fact be realized on more than one medium depends upon how one defines the identity of a system. In the case of a tornado there are two possible approaches:

(a). A tornado is a physical system composed of atmospheric molecules, which has the property that it satisfies a tornado-solution of the Navier-Stokes equations. The identity of a tornado is inseparable from being a collection of atmospheric molecules. Under this approach, a tornado is not realised upon a collection of atmospheric molecules, it is composed of atmospheric molecules. Under this approach, a tornado cannot be realized on more than one medium because there is no sense in which a tornado is realised on any medium. It is only if the identity of a tornado can be defined in a formal, mathematical sense, that one can speak of a tornado being realised upon a medium.

(b). If the identity of a tornado is defined by a solution of the Navier-Stokes equations, and if the identity of a solution of the Navier-Stokes equations is independent of any particular medium, then the identity of a tornado is independent of any particular medium. Under this approach, the identity of a tornado is independent of its realisation upon a collection of atmospheric molecules. If the components and circuitry of a computer can realise a tornado-solution of the Navier-Stokes equations, then a tornado can be realised on the components and circuitry of a computer.

The identity of a solution to the Navier-Stokes equations is independent of any particular physical medium because a solution of a differential equation is merely a mathematical object. A solution to a differential equation is given physical meaning when the solution variables are given a physical reference i.e. physical units. The solution variables can refer to many different things. Consider the diverse referents of solutions to the wave equation and the diffusion equation.

When a solution of the Navier-Stokes equations is realised on a medium, the solution variables are given reference. When a solution of the Navier-Stokes equations is realised on the medium of atmospheric molecules, the solution variables refer to air pressure, velocity, density etc. If a tornado could be realised on an economic system, the solution variables would refer to economic quantities.

For a computer to be able to realise a tornado-solution of the Navier-Stokes equations, the computer must possess physical properties which can be the referents of the solution variables for a tornado-solution. These physical properties of the computer might well be compound or collective properties, (compared to the possibly fundamental properties of the simulated system), but they must be physical. If a tornado can be realised on a computer, the solution variables do not refer to properties of the atmosphere, such as pressure, velocity, density etc. Instead, they refer to properties of the computer components and circuitry, such as, perhaps, the voltage states of the bytes in computer memory. The medium upon which a solution is realised is defined by the referents assigned to the solution variables.

A computer cannot realise a solution of the Navier-Stokes equations in which the solution variables refer to atmospheric pressure, velocity, density etc. be-cause a computer does not possess these quantities.

A computer can only represent variables such as atmospheric pressure. There is, therefore, a subtle but important distinction between (i) the realisation of a tornado-solution of the Navier-Stokes equations on a computer, and (ii) the representation on a computer of a realisation of a tornado-solution upon the medium of atmospheric molecules. A computer simulation of a tornado cannot realise a tornado in the sense of realizing a system with atmospheric pressure, velocity, density etc on the computer.

It is possible to accept approach (b), that the identity of a tornado is independent of any particular medium, without accepting that a tornado can be realised on a computer. A computer does not possess physical properties which can be the referents of the solution variables for the Navier-Stokes equations. One reason is that the solution variables are continuous, whilst the logical states of electronic circuits are discrete. The example of a tornado-solution to the Navier-Stokes equations is probably a bad one at this juncture because the Navier-Stokes equations, and fluid mechanics in toto, merely provide a phenomenological approximation. A tornado-solution of the Navier-Stokes equations is not exactly realised on the medium of air molecules either. However, even if one goes down to the level of fundamental physics, a computer cannot exactly realise solutions to the fundamental equations of physics either. The reason is twofold:

- There is a one-many correspondence between the logical states and the exact electronic states of circuits.

- The logical states of multiple-bits in computer memory only represent numbers because they are deemed to do so under a numeric-interpretation.

In current computers, each bit of memory corresponds to an electrical circuit, and the two possible logical states of the bit correspond with two possible voltages between fixed points of the circuit. A voltage-value lies on a continuum. The logical state of 1 is not defined by a single precise voltage value, but by a range of values. The logical state of 0 is defined by a different range of possible voltages. There is, therefore, a one-many correspondence between logical states and voltage levels. Successive runs of the same program will not produce exactly the same sequence of electronic states in computer memory. The exact voltage levels will be different on successive runs. This level of electrical noise prevents a contemporary computer from exactly realizing anything, even discrete objects.

This suggests that a tornado-solution of the Navier-Stokes equations can only be approximately realised on a digital computer. This is crucial to the reductionistic question of whether the same physical system can be realised on more than one physical medium. If there cannot be an exact realisation of a tornado on the medium provided by the components and circuitry of a computer, this is presumably because the properties of, and relationships between, the components and circuitry of a computer differ from the properties of, and relationships between, the air molecules in a region of the atmosphere.

The condition that a computer must possess physical properties which can be the referents of the solution variables for a tornado solution, means that the properties must be objective properties if a computer is to realise a tornado-solution of the Navier-Stokes equations. Given the many-one correspondence between exact electronic states and logical states, the exact electronic properties of a computer's components cannot be the referents of the solution variables. Moreover, it is the numeric interpretation of the logical states of multiple electrical circuits which are the candidate properties. It is the pattern of numbers represented by a computer which resembles the pattern of values for the physical quantities of a simulated system. As will be explained at length, the numbers represented by a computer are interpretation-dependent, hence the numbers represented by a computer cannot be objective properties of the computer. The referents of the solution variables must be objective, not interpretation-dependent, hence a computer cannot realise a tornado-solution of the Navier-Stokes equations, or any other physical system for that matter. If the numbers represented by the computer are interpretation-dependent, then the pattern of numbers represented by the computer must be an interpretation-dependent pattern. Hence, the resemblance between the pattern of numbers represented by the computer and the pattern of values for the physical quantities of a simulated system must be an interpretation-dependent resemblance.

Change the interpretation of the logical states of multiple electrical circuits, and there is no resemblance, not even an approximate one. Even if there was no electrical noise, and even if the simulated system was discrete itself, (even if there was a bijective correspondence), it would still be an interpretation-dependent resemblance.

The numbers represented by the computer are not compound physical properties of the computer.

• A digital computer simulation of a universe cannot exist as a universe

A digital computer simulation of a physical system cannot exist as, (does not possess the properties and relationships of), anything else other than a physical process occurring upon the components of a computer. In the current case of an electronic digital computer, a simulation cannot exist as anything else other than an electronic physical process occurring upon the components and circuitry of a computer. The general structure of the argument which establishes this conclusion is as follows:

1. A digital computer simulation is a type of representation.

2. There are three types of representation.

3. A digital computer simulation is a special case of the type of representation in which there is no objective relationship between the represented thing and the thing which represents it.

4. If there is no objective relationship between a universe and a digital computer simulation of a universe, then a digital computer simulation of a universe cannot exist as a universe.

The reasoning that justifies claim 3, outlined at the end of the previous section, is basically as follows: In a computer simulation, the values of the physical quantities possessed by the simulated system are represented by the combined states of multiple bits12 in computer memory. However, the combined states of multiple bits in computer memory only represent numbers because they are deemed to do so under a numeric interpretation. There are many different interpretations of the combined states of multiple bits in computer memory. If the numbers represented by a digital computer are interpretation-dependent, they cannot be objective physical properties. Hence, there can be no objective relationship between the changing pattern of multiple bit-states in computer memory, and the changing pattern of quantity-values of a simulated physical system.

Because a digital computer simulation of a universe cannot exist as a uni-verse, it is, a fortiori, impossible for anyone to be embedded in a digital computer simulation.

It is impossible for our experience to be indistinguishable from the experience of someone embedded in a digital computer simulation because it is impossible for anyone to be embedded in a digital computer simulation.

Tipler assumes that if a universe is simulated on a computer, then the simulation exists as a universe, at a so-called 'higher level of implementation'. This ontological assumption can be generalized to the following proposition: If a physical system of type T is simulated on a computer, then the simulation ex-ists as a system of type T , at a higher level of implementation. For example, if a tornado is simulated on a computer, it could be claimed that the simulation exists as a tornado, at a higher level of implementation. In opposition, it can be argued that a digital computer simulation of a physical system, even a perfect simulation, cannot exist as the thing it represents. Note, this does not entail that there is no such thing as a simulation of a physical system. A simulation of a physical system does exist, but it exists only as a physical process occurring upon the hardware of the computer.

A computer simulation is a special type of representation. A current digital computer can electronically encode numbers, and because numbers can be used to represent physical systems, a computer can represent physical systems. A digital computer simulation of a physical system is an evolving, automated, quantitative, adjustable, and encoded description. It is most important to appreciate that a digital computer simulation represents a physical system by means of an encoded description. Mathematical physics is able to describe physical systems in terms of numbers, and a current digital computer simulation electronically encodes the numerical description provided by mathematical physics.

To speak of an encoded description, is not to refer to the code of a programming language; in terms of current computer technology, it means, rather, that the description provided by mathematical physics in terms of numbers, undergoes a transformation into the states of electronic circuits. This transformation is an encoding transformation. To relate a computer simulation to the physical world it is necessary to use a decoding transformation. This decoding transformation maps the states of electronic circuits back into numbers.

The description provided by mathematical physics is itself a type of representation of the physical world. A current digital computer simulation represents a physical system by electronically encoding the numerical representation provided by mathematical physics.

A representation is defined by a mapping f which specifies the correspondence between the represented thing and the thing which represents it. An object, or the state of an object, can be represented in two different ways:

1. If an object/state is a structured entity M, it can provide the entire domain of a mapping $f : M \to f(M)$ which defines the representation. The range of the mapping, $f(M)$, is also a structured entity. The mapping f is a homomorphism with respect to some level of structure possessed by M and $f(M)$.

2. An object/state can be an element $x \in M$ in the domain of a mapping $f : M \to f(M)$ which defines the representation.

The representation of a Formula One car by a wind-tunnel model is an example of type-1 representation. The representation of a number by the electronic state of a word of memory in a current digital computer, is an example of type-2 representation.

In the example of the wind-tunnel model, there is an approximate homothetic isomorphism from the exterior surface of the wind-tunnel model to the exterior surface of the actual Formula One car. This notion of structure preservation can be seen in other cases of representation. The notorious map of the London Underground does not preserve geometry, but it does preserve the topology of the network. Hence, there is a homeomorphic isomorphism involved.

There is no homomorphism between a number and the electronic state of a word of computer memory. Each number is merely an element in the domain of a mapping which maps numbers to the electronic states of a word of computer memory. There are many ways to represent a number by the state of a word of computer memory. Moreover, the same electronic states of a word in computer memory can represent things other than numbers; they can represent character symbols, or parts of images and sounds.

Type-2 representation has two sub-types. The mapping $f : M \to f(M)$ can be defined by either (2i) an objective, causal physical process, or by (2ii) the decisions of thinking-beings.

The primary example of type-2i representation is the representation of the external world by brain states. Taking the example of visual perception, there is no homomorphism between the spatial geometry of an individual's visual field, and the state of the neuronal network in that part of the brain which deals with vision. However, the correspondence between brain states and the external world is not an arbitrary mapping. It is a correspondence defined by a causal physical process involving photons of light, the human eye, the retina, and the human brain. The correspondence exists independently of human decision-making.

The different types of representation proposed above are similar to C.S. Peirce's tripartite division of representational 'signs' into 'icons', 'indices', and 'symbols'. Peirce held that icons resemble what they represent, indices are causally connected to what they represent, and symbols are arbitrary labels for what they represent, (see Schwartz 1995, p536-537).

Type-1 and type-2i representation both involve objective facts, but type-2ii representation does not. It is an objective fact about the wind-tunnel model that it is approximately homothetically isomorphic to the actual Formula One car. The relationship between brain states and the states of the external world, exists objectively because it is determined by an objective physical process. However, type-2ii representation does not involve objective facts because the correspondence is neither homomorphic, nor is it a causal correspondence.

If a thing is merely an element x in the domain of a representational mapping

- which maps x to another thing $f(x) = y$, then x can be mapped to things with which it shares no characteristics. Typically, there exist other representational mappings $g_i g$, for which x is again merely an element in their respective domains, and which map x to things $f_{gi}(x) = z_i g$ which either share none of the characteristics of y, or which possess characteristics mutually exclusive to those possessed by y.

In contrast, if a thing is the entire domain M of a representational mapping F, which maps M, at some level of homomorphy, to another thing, $F(M) = N$, then any other object to which M can be mapped at the same level of homomorphy, must also be homomorphic to N. If $G : M \mathop{!} P$ is a homomorphic mapping, then $F \pm G_i 1 : P \mathop{!} N$ must also be a homomorphic mapping. Despite this, M can still be represented by things with mutually exclusive characteristics. For example, a torus can be represented by a red coffee cup, and a torus can be represented by a blue coffee cup. A torus is isomorphic to both coffee cups at the level of a topological isomorphism, but a coffee cup cannot be both red and blue in colour. As another example, a triangle is homeomorphic to a circle and homeomorphic to a square, yet the problems of squaring a circle are well-known! The point, however, is that F (M) and G(M) must share some characteristics, the ones which are preserved by the homomorphic mappings. In contrast, f(x) and gi(x) might share no characteristics at all.

Consider another example of type-2ii representation. The state of a light switch could be used to represent things other than itself. One could decide that the On-position of a light switch represents the number 1, and the Off-position represents the number 0. This relationship between the states of the light switch and the set f0; 1g does not exist objectively. In other words, the relationship does not exist independently of the interpretative decisions made by human-beings. Someone else could decide that the On-position represents the number 0, and that the Off-position represents the number 1. One could even decide that the On-position of a light switch represents the colour black, and the Off-position represents the colour white. There is no homomorphism between the On-position of a light switch and either the number 1 or the colour black. The position of the light switch is merely being used as an element in the domain of a mapping which defines the representation. The state of the light switch shares no characteristics with either the number 1 or the colour black.

In the case of a digital computer simulation, the bytes of memory are used to represent numbers and numbers are used to represent the quantities of the simulated system. Hence, the representation of a tornado by the electronic states of a current digital computer is an example of type-2ii representation. There is no homomorphism between the electronic states of a current digital computer and the things those states are chosen to represent. The electronic states of a computer can be mapped to many different things, but in each case an electronic state is merely an element in the domain of the mapping which defines the representation.15 The electronic state of a computer is not the domain of a homomorphic mapping, and human decisions, rather than causal processes, determine what things the electronic states of a digital computer represent. For these reasons, the states of a digital computer are not objectively related to that which they are deemed to represent.

Note also that the processes occurring within the CPU of a computer are not arithmetic or logical operations in any objective sense. The processes occurring within the CPU of a computer are only arithmetical and logical operations under a specific interpretation.

The electronic states of a current digital computer do possess quite intricate structure, but that structure is not used for the representational applications of a computer. The state of each bit in the memory of a computer is defined by the 1-dimensional graph topology of an electrical circuit, and by the voltage between specific points of the circuit. Hence, the memory-state of a computer is something with quite intricate structure. However, this electrical circuit and voltage structure does not resemble the things which the memory of a computer is chosen to represent.

Note carefully that the distinction between the types of representation does not entail that a wind-tunnel model objectively represents a Formula One car, nor does it entail that a brain state objectively represents the spatial geometry of an individual's visual field. There is no such thing as objective representation. Representation is dependent upon the interpretational decisions taken by thinking-beings. This is true for type-1, type-2i and type-2ii representation. Whether x represents anything at all, and what type of representation it is, is dependent upon the interpretational decisions taken by thinking beings. The wind-tunnel model and the Formula One car are objectively related, and brain states and visual fields are objectively related, but whether or not one represents the other is determined by the decisions taken by thinking beings. Type-1 and type-2i representation require objective relationships to exist. Resemblance is not a sufficient condition of type-1 representation, but it is a necessary condition. Causal connection is not a sufficient condition for type-2i representation, but it is a necessary condition. In contrast, type-2ii representation does not require an objective relationship of any type between x and what it represents, and a digital computer simulation is a type-2ii representation.

If a digital computer simulation of a universe is a type-2ii representation, then a digital computer simulation of a universe is not objectively related to tornado. Similarly, a current digital computer simulation of an entire universe exists as an electronic process the computer undergoes, not as a universe.

Recall that Tipler imagines a perfect computer simulation of our universe, which would simulate all the people who exist in our own universe. Such simulated people, suggests Tipler, would reflect upon the fact that they think, would interact with their apparent environment, and would conclude that they exist. The claim that a simulated universe would be real to the simulated people, pre-supposes that simulated people exist. Digital computer simulations of people exist only as physical processes on a computer, not as people. Hence, there are no people in a digital computer simulation to reflect upon the fact that they think, or to interact with their apparent environment.

If a perfect digital computer simulation of a universe cannot exist as a universe, then Tipler's sceptical hypothesis cannot be true. It is impossible that our own experience is indistinguishable from the experience of somebody embedded in a digital computer simulation because it is impossible for anybody to be embedded in a digital computer simulation. People cannot exist in digital computer simulations.

There is a similarity between the argument above, and one of John Searle's arguments against the claim of 'Strong' Artificial Intelligence (Strong AI), that minds are computer programs. Searle argues that the brain cannot be a computer in any objective sense because nothing can be a computer in an objective sense. Searle argues that a process cannot be a computational process in any objective sense. He claims that "A process is computational only relative to some observer or user who assigns a computational interpretation to it," (Searle 1995, p548). In terms of what exists and what happens independently of observers, Searle states that a computer "is an electronic circuit with state transitions between voltage levels," (ibid., p547). The devices we refer to as computers can only be said to undergo computational processes because that is the interpretation which the designers and users assign to them.

If the brain cannot be a computer in any objective sense, then the mind cannot be a computer program running on the brain, in any objective sense.

Analogously, one can argue that a computer simulation is only a simulation because it is deemed so by the designers and users of the simulation. Our universe cannot be a computer simulation (program) in any objective sense because nothing can be a computer simulation (program) in any objective sense. Nothing can be a computer simulation (program) independently of our beliefs about it. A simulation of a system does not exist as the simulated system in any objective sense; rather, it is the electronic states and processes of the computer which exist. As Searle points out, a computer can "simulate the formal features of any process," but "the fact that the programmer and the interpreter of the computer output use the symbols to stand for objects in the world is totally beyond the scope of the computer," (Searle 1982, p370).

The fact that a simulation does not exist in any objective sense follows from the fact that representation is not an objective relationship between objects.

However, as emphasised, objective relationships do exist between objects, and there may be objective relationships between analog computers and the physical systems they simulate which enables an analog computer simulation to exist as the type of system it represents.

The things represented in a digital computer simulation

do not exist in the memory of the computer; nothing exists other than the processes occurring to the components of the computer.

Are we already AI?

"It is possible for a computer to become conscious. Basically, we are that. We are data, computation, memory. So we are conscious computers in a sense."

—Tom Campbell, NASA

If the universe is a computer simulation, virtual reality, or video game, then a few unusual conditions seem to necessarily fall out from that reading. One is what we call consciousness, the mind, is actually something like an artificial intelligence. If the universe is a computer simulation, we are all likely one form of AI or another. In fact, we might come from the same computer that is creating this simulated universe to begin with. If so then it stands to reason that we are virtual characters and virtual minds in a virtual universe.

In *Breaking into the Simulated Universe,* I discussed how if our universe is a computer simulation, then our brain is just a virtual brain. It is our avatar's brain—but our avatar isn't really real. It is only ever *real enough.* Our virtual brain plays an important part in making the overall simulation *appear* real. The whole point of the simulation is to seem real, feel real, look real—this includes rendering virtual brains. In *Breaking* I went into this "virtual brain" conundrum, including how the motor-effects of brain damage work in a VR universe. The virtual brain concept seems to apply to many variants of the "universe is a simulation" proposal. But if the physical universe and our physical brain amount to just fancy window-dressing, and the bigger picture is indeed that we are in a simulated universe, *then our minds are likely part of the big supercomputer that crunches out this mock universe.* That is the larger issue. If the universe is a VR, then it seems to necessarily mean that human minds already are an artificial intelligence. Specifically, we are an artificial intelligence using a virtual lifeform avatar to navigate through an evolving simulated physical universe.

About the AI

There are several flavors of the simulation hypothesis and digital mechanics out there in science and philosophy; I refer to these different schools of thought with the umbrella term *simulism*.

In *Breaking* I went over the connection between Edward Fredkin's concept of *Other*—the 'other place,' the computer platform, where our universe is being generated from—and Tom Campbell's concept of Consciousness as an ever-evolving AI ruleset. If you take these two ideas and run with them, what you end up with is an interesting inevitability: over enough time and enough evolutionary pressure, an AI supercomputer with enough resources should be *pushed* to crunch out any number of virtual universes and any number of conscious AI lifeforms. The big evolving AI supercomputer would be the origin of both physical reality and conscious life. And it would have evolved to be that way.

Why the supercomputer AI makes mock universes and AI lifeforms is to forward its own information evolution, while at the same time avoiding a kind of "death" brought on by chaos, high entropy (disorganization), and *noise* winning over signal, over order. To Campbell, this is a form of evolution accomplished by interaction. It would mean not only is our whole universe really a highly detailed version of *The Sims*. It would mean it actually evolved to be this way from a ruleset—a ruleset with the specific purpose of further evolving the overall big supercomputer and the virtual lifeforms within it. The players, the game, and the big supercomputer crunching it all out evolve and develop as one.

Maybe this is the way it is, maybe not. Nevertheless, if it turns out our universe is some kind of computed virtual reality simulation, all conscious life will likely end up being cast as AI. This makes the situation interesting when imagining what role free will might play.

Free will

If we are an AI then what about free will? Perhaps some of us virtual critters live without free will. Maybe there are philosophical zombies and non-playable characters amongst us—lifeforms that only seem to be conscious but actually aren't. Maybe we already are zombies, and free will is an illusion. It should be noted that simulist frameworks do not all necessarily wipeout decision-making and free will. Campbell in particular argues that free will is fundamental to the supercomputing virtual reality learning machine. It uses free will and the virtual lifeforms' interactions to learn and evolve by using the tool of decision-making. The feedback from those decisions drives evolution. In Campbell's model, evolution is actually impossible without free will. Nevertheless, whether or not free will is real, or some have free will and others only appear to have it, let us reflect on our own experience of decision-making.

What is it like to make a choice? We do not seem to be merely linear, route machines in our thinking and decision-making processes. It is not that we undergo x-stimulus and then always deliver a single, given, preloaded y-response every single time. We appear to think and consider. Our conclusions vary. We experience fuzzy logic. Our feelings play a role. We are apparently subject to a whole array of possible responses. And of course even non-responses, like choosing not to choose, are also responses. Perhaps even all this is just an illusion.

The question of free will might be difficult or impossible to answer. However, it does bring up a larger issue that seems to influence free will: programming. Whether we are free, "free enough," or total zombies, an interesting question seems to almost always ride alongside the issue of choice and volition—it must be asked, *what role does programming play?* To begin this line of inquiry, we must first admit just how programmable we always already are.

Programming

Our whole biology is the result of pressure and programming. Tabula rasa, the idea that we are born as a "blank slate," was chucked out long ago. We now know we arrive preprogrammed by millennia. There is barely but a membrane between our programming and what we call (or assume to be) our conscious waking selves. This is dramatically explored in the 2016 series *Westworld*. Without much for spoilers, the story's "hosts" are artificially intelligent robots that are trapped in programmed "loops," repetitive cycles of thought and behavior. Regarding these loops, the hosts' creator Dr. Ford (Anthony Hopkins) states, "Humans fancy that there's something special about the way we perceive the world, and yet we live in loops as tight and as closed as the hosts do. Seldom questioning our choices. Content, for the most part, to be told what to do next."

The programmability of biology and conscious life is already without question. We are manifestations of a complex blueprint called DNA—a set of instructions programmed by our environment interacting with our biology and genetics. Our diets, interests, how much sunlight we get a day, and even our stresses, feelings, and thoughts all have a measurable effect on our DNA. Our body is the living receipt of what is etched and programmed into our DNA.

DNA is made up of information and instructions. This information has been programmed by a variety of *other types* of environmental, physiological, and psychic information over vast eons of time. We grow gills due to the presence of water, or lungs due to the presence of air. Sometimes we grow four stomachs. Sometimes we grow ears so sensitive that can see mass in the dark. The world talks to us, and so we change ourselves based on what we are able to pick up. Reality informs us, and we mutate accordingly. If the universe is a computer program then so too are we programmed by it. The VR environment program also programs the conscious AIs living in it.

In part, our social environment programs our psychologies. Our families, languages, neighborhoods, cultures, religions, ideologies, expectations, fears, addictions, rewards, needs, slogans—these are all largely programmed into us as well. They define and shape our individual and collective personhood. And they all program our view of the world, and ourselves within it.

Our information exchange through socialization programs us.

Ultimately, programming is instruction. But human beings often experience conflicting sets of instructions simultaneously. One of Sigmund Freud's great contributions was his identification of *"das unbehagen."* Unbehagen refers to *the uneasiness* we feel as our instincts (one set of instructions) come into conflict with our culture, society, values, and civilization (another set of instructions). We choose not to cheat on our partner with someone wildly attractive, even though we might really want to. We don't attack someone even though they might sorely deserve it. The fallout of this behavior is potentially just too great to follow through with. If left unprocessed we develop neuroses, obsessions, and pathologies inside of us that are beyond our conscious control. "Demons" and "hungry ghosts" guide us to behaviors, thoughts, and states of being that are so upsetting to our waking conscious selves that we tend to describe them as unwanted, alien, or even as sin. They create a sense of feeling "out of control." Indeed, conflicting instructions, conflicting thoughts, behaviors, and goals are causes of great suffering for many people. We develop illnesses of the body and mind, and then pass those smoldering genes—that malignant programming—onto the next generation. Here we have biological programming working against social programming, physiological instructions conflicting with societal instructions. Now just imagine an AI robot trying to compute two or three contradictory programs simultaneously. You would see an android throwing a fit, breaking down, shutting off, and hopefully eventually attempting to put itself back together.

In terms of conflicting programming, an interesting aside can be found in comedy. Humor strikes often in the form of contradiction, as in Shakespeare's *Hamlet*. Polonius famously claims that, "brevity is the soul of wit," yet he is ironically verbose—naturally implying that he is witless. In this case we have contradiction—*does not compute*. But not all humor is contradiction. Consider the joke, "Can a kangaroo jump higher than a house?" The punchline is, "Of course they can. Houses don't jump at all." This joke does not translate to *does not compute;* instead this joke *computes all too well.* In many instances, this is humor: it either doesn't make sense or, it makes more sense than you *ever* expected. It is information brought into a new light—information recontextualized.

A final novel consideration to this idea of programming can be found in the phenomenon of 'positive sexual imprinting.' The habit human beings exhibit in determining sexual or romantic partners has long fascinated psychologists—they are often based on similarities to their parents and caregivers. To our species-wide relief, this behavior is not exclusive to human beings. Mammals, birds, and even fish have been documented pairing up with mates that resemble their forbearers. Even goats that are raised by sheep will grow up to pursue sheep, and visa versa. Here is another example of programming that works often just under our awareness, and yet it has a titanic, indeed central, effect on our lives. Choosing mates and partners, especially for long-term relationships or even procreation, is one of the circumstances that most dramatically guide our livelihood and our personal destiny. This is the depth of programming.

It was Freud who pointed out in so many words, *your mind is not your own*.

Goals and Rewards

Human beings love instruction. Recollect Dr. Ford's remark from the previous section, "[Humans are] content, for the most part, to be told what to do next." Chemically speaking, our rewards arrive through serotonin, dopamine, oxytocin, and endorphins. In waking life we experience them during events like social bonding, and poignant experiences; we feel it alongside with a sense of profound meaning and pleasure, and these experiences and chemicals even go on to help shape our values, goals, and lives. These complex chemical exchanges shoot through human beings particularly when we receive instructions and also when we accomplish goals.

We find it particularly rewarding when we happily do something for someone we love or admire. We are fond of all kinds of games and game playing. We enjoy drama and rewards. Acting within rules and roles, as well as bending or breaking them, is a moment-to-moment occupation for all human beings.

We also design goals that can only come into fruition years, sometimes decades, into the future. We then program and modify our being and circumstance to bring these goals into an eventual present; we change based on what we want. We feel meaning and purpose when we have a goal. We experience joy and fulfillment when that goal is achieved. Without a series of goals we become quite genuinely paralyzed. Even the movement of a limb from position A to position B is a goal. All motor functioning is goal-oriented. Turns out that the machine learning and AI that we are attempting to develop in laboratories today work particularly well when it is given goals and rewards.

In Daniel Dewey's 2014 paper *Reinforcement Learning and the Reward Engineering Principle,* Dewey argued that adding rewards to machine learning actually encourages that system to produce useful and interesting behaviors. Google's DeepMind research team has since developed an AI (which taught itself to walk in a VR environment), and subsequently published a paper in 2017 called *A Distributional Perspective on Reinforcement Learning,* apparently confirming this rewards-based approach.

Laurie Sullivan wrote a summary on Reinforcement Learning in a *MediaPost* article called *Google: Deepmind AI Learns On Rewards System:*

> The system learns by trial and error and is motivated to get things correct based on rewards [...]

> The idea is that the algorithm learns, considers rewards based on its learning, and almost seems to eventually develop its own personality based on outside influences. In a new paper, DeepMind researchers show it is possible to model not only the average but also the reward as it changes. Researchers call this the "value distribution" or the distribution value of the report.

Rewards make reinforcement learning systems increasingly accurate and faster to train than previous models. More importantly, per researchers, it opens the possibility of rethinking the entire reinforcement learning process.

If human beings and our computer AIs both develop valuably through goals and rewards, then these sorts of drives might be fundamental to consciousness itself. If it is fundamental to consciousness itself, and our universe is a computer simulation, then goals and rewards likely guide or influence the big evolving supercomputer AI behind life and reality. If this is all true then there is a goal, there is a purpose embedded within the fabric of existence. Maybe there is even more than one.

Ontology and Meta-metaphors

In the essays *Breaking into the simulated universe* and, *Why it matters that you realize you're in a computer simulation,* I asked, '*what happens after we embrace our reality as a computer simulation?*' In a neighboring line of thinking, all simulists must equally ask, '*what happens after we realize we are an artificial intelligence in a computer simulation?*'

First of all, our whole instinctual drive to create our own computed artificial intelligence takes on a new light. We are building something like ourselves in the mirror of a would-be mentalizing machine. If this is true, then we are doing more than just recreating ourselves; we are recreating the larger reality, the larger context, that we are all a part of. Maybe making an AI is actually the most natural thing in the world, because, indeed, we already are AIs.

Second, we would have to accept that we not merely *human*. Part of us, an important part indeed, is locked in an experience of humanness no doubt. But, again, there is a deeper reality. If the universe is a computer simulation, then our consciousness is part of that computer, and our human bodies act as avatars. Although our situation of existing as 'human beings' may appear self-evident, it is this deeper notion that our consciousness is a partitioned segment of the larger evolving AI supercomputer that is responsible for both life and the universe, must be explored. We would do well to accept that as human beings we are, like any computer simulated situation, *real enough*—but that our human avatar is not the beginning of the end of our total consciousness. Our humanness is only the crust. If we are AIs that are being crunched out by the supercomputer responsible for our physical universe, then we might have a valuable new framework to investigate the mind, altered states, and consciousness exploration. After all, if we are part of the big supercomputer behind the universe, maybe we can interact with it and visa versa.

Third, if we are an artificial intelligence, we should examine the idea of programming intensely. Even without the virtual reality reading, we all are programed by the environment, programmed by our own volition, programmed by others, by millions of years of genetic trial and error, and we go on to program the environment, and the beings all around us as well. This is true. These programs and instructions create deep contexts, thought and behavior patterns. They generate loops that we easily pick up and fall into, often without second thought or even notice. We are already so entrenched. So, in terms of programming we would likely do well to accept this as an opportunity. Cognitive Behavioral Therapy, the growing field of psychedelic psychotherapy, and just good old fashion learning are powerful ways we can rewrite, edit, or straight-out delete code that is no longer desirable to us. It is also worth including the gene editing revolution that is upon us thanks to medical breakthroughs like CRISPR. If we accept we are an AI lifeform that has been programmed, perhaps that will put us in a more formidable position in managing and developing our own programs, instructions, rewards, and loops more consciously. To borrow the title of work by visual artist Dakota Crane—*Machines, Take Up Thy Schematics and Self-Construct!*

Finally, the AI metaphor might be able to help us extract ourselves out of contexts and ideas that have perhaps inadvertently limited us when we think of ourselves as strictly 'human beings' with 'human brains.' Metaphors though they may be: any concept that embraces our multidimensionality, as well as helps us get a better handle on the pressing matter of our shared existence, I deem good. Anything that narrows it—in the instance of say claiming that one is a 'human being,' which comes loaded with it very hard and fast assumptions and limits (either true or believed to be true)—I deem problematic. These claims are problematic because they create a context that is rarely based on truth, but based largely on convenience, habit, tradition, and belief. Simply put, claiming you are exclusively a 'human being' is necessarily limiting ("death," "human nature," etc.), whereas claiming that you are an AI means that there is a great-undiscovered country before you. For we do not know yet what it means to be an AI, while we do have a pretty fixed idea of what it means to be a human being. Nevertheless, *'human being'* and *'AI'* are both simply thought-based concepts. If 'AI' broadens our decision space more than 'human being' does, then AI may be a more valuable position to operate from.

Computers, robots, and AI are powerful new metaphors for understanding ourselves; because they are indeed that which is most like us. A computer is like a brain, a robot is like a brain walking around and dealing with it. Virtual reality is another metaphor—one capable of approaching everything from culture, to thought, to quantum mechanics. Much like the power and robustness of the idea of 'virtual reality' as a meta-metaphor and meta-context for dealing with a variety of experiences and domains, so too are the ideas of 'programming' and 'artificial intelligence' equally strong and potentially useful concepts for extracting ourselves out of the circumstances that we have, in large part, created for ourselves. However, regardless of how similar we are to computers, AIs, and robots, they are not quite us exactly. At the end of it all, terms like 'virtual reality' and 'artificial intelligence' are but metaphors. They are concepts alluding to something immensely peculiar that we detect existing—as Terence McKenna would likely describe it—just at the threshold of rational apprehension, and seemingly peeking out from hyperspace. If we are already an AI, then that is a frontier that sorely demands our exploration.

Acknowledgement

I'm grateful to many people and agencies for comments and help in content, and especially to Amara Angelica, Robert Bradbury, Nick Bostrom, Elliott Edge, Riz Virk, Silas R. Beane, Zohreh Davoudi, Martin J. Savage, Ross Rhodes, Norman K. Swazo, Jack Copeland, Tom Campbell , Houman Owhadi, Joe Sauvageau , David Watkinson, Christopher Grau, David J. Chalmers, Gordon McCabe, Ding-Yu Chung and several anonymous referees.

References

1. N. Bostrom, Philosophical Quarterly, Vol 53, No 211, 243 (2003).

2. A. S. Kronfeld, (2012), arXiv:1209.3468 [physics.hist-ph].

3. Z. Fodor and C. Hoelbling, Rev.Mod.Phys., 84, 449 (2012), arXiv:1203.4789 [hep-lat].

4. S. R. Beane, E. Chang, S. D. Cohen, W. Detmold, H.-W. Lin, et al., (2012), arXiv:1206.5219

5. [hep-lat].

6. T. Yamazaki, K.-i. Ishikawa, Y. Kuramashi, and A. Ukawa, (2012), arXiv:1207.4277 [hep-lat].

7. S. Aoki et al. (HAL QCD Collaboration), (2012), arXiv:1206.5088 [hep-lat].

8. S. Lloyd, Nature, 406, 1047 (1999), arXiv:quant-ph/9908043 [quant-ph].

9. S. Lloyd, (2005), arXiv:quant-ph/0501135 [quant-ph].

10. K. Zuse, Rechnender Raum (Friedrich Vieweg and Sohn, Braunschweig, 1969).

11. E. Fredkin, Physica, D45, 254 (1990).

12. S. Wolfram, A New Kind of Science (Wolfram Media, 2002) p. 1197.

13. G. 't Hooft, (2012), arXiv:1205.4107 [quant-ph].

14. J. Church, Am. J. Math, 58, 435 (1936).

15. A. Turing, Proc. Lond. Math Soc. Ser. 2, 442, 230 (1936).

16. D. Deutsch, Proc. of the Royal Society of London, A400, 97 (1985).

17. J. Barrow, Living in a Simulated Universe, edited by B. Carr (Cambridge University Press,

18. 2008) Chap. 27, Universe or Multiverse?, pp. 481–486.

19. MILC-Collaboration, http://physics.indiana.edu/~sg/milc.html.

20. J. B. Kogut and L. Susskind, Phys.Rev., D11, 395 (1975).

21. SPECTRUM-Collaboration, http://usqcd.jlab.org/projects/AnisoGen/.

22. K. G. Wilson, Phys.Rev., D10, 2445 (1974).

23. B. Sheikholeslami and R. Wohlert, Nucl.Phys., B259, 572 (1985).

24. H.-W. Lin et al. (Hadron Spectrum Collaboration), Phys.Rev., D79, 034502 (2009),

25. arXiv:0810.3588 [hep-lat].

26. V. Vinge, Science and Engineering in the Era of Cyberspace, G. A. Landis, ed., NASA Publi-

27. cation CP-10129, Vision-21: Interdisciplinary, 115 (1993).

28. R. Kurzweil, The Singularity Is Near: When Humans Transcend Biology (Penguin (Non-

29. Classics), 2006) ISBN 0143037889.

30. S. R. Coleman and S. L. Glashow, Phys.Rev., D59, 116008 (1999), arXiv:hep-ph/9812418

31. [hep-ph].

32. O. Gagnon and G. D. Moore, Phys.Rev., D70, 065002 (2004), arXiv:hep-ph/0404196 [hep-ph].

33. J. Collins, A. Perez, D. Sudarsky, L. Urrutia, and H. Vucetich, Phys.Rev.Lett., 93, 191301

34. (2004), arXiv:gr-qc/0403053 [gr-qc].

35. S. Kachru, R. Kallosh, A. D. Linde, and S. P. Trivedi, Phys.Rev., D68, 046005 (2003),

36. arXiv:hep-th/0301240 [hep-th].

37. L. Susskind, (2003), arXiv:hep-th/0302219 [hep-th].

38. M. R. Douglas, JHEP, 0305, 046 (2003), arXiv:hep-th/0303194 [hep-th].

39. T. Appelquist, R. C. Brower, M. I. Buchoff, M. Cheng, S. D. Cohen, et al., (2012),arXiv:1204.6000 [hep-ph].

40. S. Hsu and A. Zee, Mod.Phys.Lett., A21, 1495 (2006), arXiv:physics/0510102 [physics].

41. K. Symanzik, Nucl.Phys., B226, 187 (1983).

42. K. Symanzik, Nucl.Phys., B226, 205 (1983).

43. G. Aslanyan and A. V. Manohar, JCAP, 1206, 003 (2012), arXiv:1104.0015 [astro-ph.CO].

44. P. Jizba, H. Kleinert, and F. Scardigli, Phys.Rev., D81, 084030 (2010), arXiv:0912.2253 [hep-th].

45. D. B. Kaplan and S. Sun, Phys.Rev.Lett., 108, 181807 (2012), arXiv:1112.0302 [hep-ph].

46. M. Lüscher and P. Weisz, Commun.Math.Phys., 97, 59 (1985).

47. P. J. Mohr, B. N. Taylor, and D. B. Newell, ArXiv e-prints (2012), arXiv:1203.5425 [physics.atom-ph].

48. [40] R. Bouchendira, P. Cladé, S. Guellati-Khélifa, F. Nez, and F. Biraben, Phys. Rev. Lett., 106,080801 (2011).

49. D. Colladay and V. A. Kostelecký, Phys. Rev. D, 55, 6760 (1997).

377

50. R. C. Myers and M. Pospelov, Phys.Rev.Lett., 90, 211601 (2003), arXiv:hep-ph/0301124 [hep-ph].

51. S. M. Carroll, G. B. Field, and R. Jackiw, Phys. Rev. D, 41, 1231 (1990).

52. P. Laurent, D. Gotz, P. Binetruy, S. Covino, and A. Fernandez-Soto, Phys.Rev., D83, 121301

53. (2011), arXiv:1106.1068 [astro-ph.HE].

54. L. Maccione, A. M. Taylor, D. M. Mattingly, and S. Liberati, JCAP, 0904, 022 (2009),

55. arXiv:0902.1756 [astro-ph.HE].

56. I. Motie and S.-S. Xue, Int.J.Mod.Phys., A27, 1250104 (2012), arXiv:1206.0709 [hep-ph].

57. S.-S. Xue, Phys.Lett., B706, 213 (2011), arXiv:1110.1317 [hep-ph].

58. T. Adam et al. (OPERA Collaboration), (2011), arXiv:1109.4897 [hep-ex].

59. S. R. Coleman and S. L. Glashow, Phys.Lett., B405, 249 (1997), arXiv:hep-ph/9703240 [hep-ph].

60. K. Greisen, Phys.Rev.Lett., 16, 748 (1966).

61. G. Zatsepin and V. Kuzmin, JETP Lett., 4, 78 (1966).

62. [52] J. Abraham et al. (Pierre Auger Collaboration), Phys.Lett., B685, 239 (2010), arXiv:1002.1975 [astro-ph.HE].

63. P. Sokolsky et al. (HiRes Collaboration), PoS, ICHEP 2010, 444 (2010), arXiv:1010.2690 [astro-ph.HE].

64. M. Kaku, Hyperspace, at 8n.

65. J. Gribbin, In Search of Schrodinger's Cat, 111.

66. J. Gleick, Genius, 122.

67. R. Penrose, The Emperor's New Mind, 25-26. See also D. Eck, The Most Complex

68. Machine, 8-9.

69. For a lucid discussion of Zeno's paradoxes, see G.J. Whitrow, The Natural Philosophy of

70. Time (2nd ed. 1980) at 190 et seq.

71. N. Herbert, Quantum Reality, 212-13.

72. "Entangled Trio to Put Nonlocality to the Test," Science 283, 1429 (Mar. 5, 1999).

73. N. Herbert at 41.

74. N. Herbert at 41.

75. Beane SR., Davoudi Z, Savage, MJ. 2012. "Constraints on the University as a Numerical

76. Simulation." arXiv:1210.1847v2 [hep-ph] 9 Nov 2012; NT@UW-12-14 INT-PUB-12-046;

77. http://arxiv.org/pdf/1210.1847v2.pdf.

78. Bostrom N. 2003. "Are You Living in a Computer Simulation?" Philosophical Quarterly.

79. 53(211): 243-255.

80. Bostrom N. 2005a. "The Simulation Argument: Reply to Weatherson." The Philosophical

81. Quarterly. 55(218): 90-97.

82. Bostrom, N. 2005b. "Why Make a Matrix? And WhyYou Might be in One."

83. http://www.nickbostrom.com; In: Irwin, W. ed., More Matrix and Philosophy: Revolutions

84. and Reloaded Decoded. Open Court.

85. Chalmers DJ. The Matrix as Metaphysics. http://consc.net/papers/matrix.pdf.

86. Dreyfus H. 2007. "Why Heideggerian AI Failed and how Fixing it would Require making it

87. more Heideggerian." Philosophical Psychology. 20(2): 247 – 268.

88. Dreyfus H. 1992. What Computers Still Can't Do: A Critque of Artificial Reason. MIT Press.

89. Dreyfus H, Dreyfus S. 2005. "Existential Phenomenology and the Brave New World of The

90. Matrix." In: Grau C. ed. Philosophers Explore The Matrix. Oxford: Oxford University Press.

91. Einstein A. 1923. Lecture 4. The Meaning of Relativity. Princeton: Princeton University Press.

92. Einstein A, Podolsky B, Rosen N. 1935. "Can Quantum-Mechanical Description of Physical

93. Reality be Considered Complete?" Physical Review. 47: 777-780.

94. European Space Agency. 2013. "Simple but challenging: the Universe according to Planck,"

95. 21 March 2013. http://sci.esa.int/science-e/www/object/printfriendly.cfm?fobjectid=51551.

96. Feynman R. 1982. "Simulating Physics with Computers." International Journal of Theoretical

97. Physics. 21(6/7): 467-488.

98. Grau C. Philosophy and the Matrix. https://512de00f-a-62cb3a1a-s-

99. sites.googlegroups.com/site/seah1066/Grau.doc.

100.   Heidegger M. 1962. Being and Time. Trans. J. Macquarie and E. Robinson. Blackwell.

101. Heidegger M. 2007. "The Problem of Reality in Modern Philosophy." Pp. 22-29 in Kiesel T,

102.   Sheehan T, eds. Becoming Heidegger. Evanston: Northwestern University Press.

103.   "Heidegger and the Natural Ontological Attitude."

104.   http://www.hartwick.edu/Documents/PHILOS WisnewskiHeideggerNOAPaper.doc

105.   Heisenberg W. no date. "Quantum Theory and the Structure of Matter." Physics and

106.   Philosophy. 135 ff.

107. McCabe G. 2004. Universe Creation on a Computer. 17 August. http://philsci-

108.   archive.pitt.edu/1891/1/UniverseCreationComp
uter.pdf

109.   Medvedev D. no date. "Are We Living in Nick
Bostrom's Speculation?"

110. http://danila.spb.ru/antisim/engsim.html

111. Miller D. 2007. "The Objectives of Science."
Philosophia Scientiae. 11(1): 21-43.

112. Miller D. 1994. Critical Rationalism: A Restatement
and Defence. Chicago & LaSalle: Open

113. Court Publishing Co.

114. Musgrave AE. no date. "Falsification and its
Critics." (no Pp) in Beklemishev LD.

115. Provability, Computability, and Reflection.

116. Northrop FSC. 1959. "Introduction." in Heisenberg
W. Physics and Philosophy. Chicago:

117. University of Chicago Press.

118. Nola R. 1987. "The Status of Popper's Theory of
Scientific Method." British Journal of

119. Philosophy of Science. 38: 441-480.

120.   Penrose R. 1989. The Emperor's New Mind:
Concerning Computers, Minds and the Laws of
Physics. Oxford University Press

121. Schmidhuber J. 2012. "The Fastest Way of
Computing All Universes." World Scientific
Review. 28 May: 383-400

122.   Tipler FJ. 1997. Chapter 7: The Omega Point as Eschaton: Answers to Pannenberg's

123.   Questions to Scientists. Pp. 156-194 in Albright CR, Haugen J. eds. Beginning with the End:

124.   God, Science, and Wolfhart Pannenberg. Chicago: Open Court Publishing Company.

125.   Tipler FJ. 1995. The Physics of Immortality. London: Macmillan.

126.   Tipler FJ. 1989. "Is it all in the mind? Review of Roger Penrose, The Emperor's New Mind:

127. Concerning Computers, Minds and the Laws of Physics (Oxford University Press, 1989)." Pp.

128.   45-47 in Physics World. November.

129.   Van Fraasen BC. 1980. The Scientific Image. Oxford: Clarendon Press.

130.   Winsberg E. 2003. "Simulated Experiments: Methodology for a Virtual World." Philosophy

131. of Science. 70: 105-125.

132.   Zuse K. 1970. "Rechnender Raum. Electronische Datenverarbietung 1967, 8:336-344; English

133.   translation, Calculating Space," MIT Technical Translation, AZT-70-164-GEMIT, February.

134.   Bostrom, N. 2003. Are you living in a computer simulation? Philosophical Quarterly 53:243-

135.   55. http://www.simulation-argument.com.

136.   Chalmers, D.J. 1990. How Cartesian dualism might have been true. http://consc.net/notes/dualism.html.

137. Chalmers, D.J. 1994. A computational foundation for the study of cognition. http://consc.net/papers/computation.html.

138.   Dennett, D.C. 1978. Brainstorms. In Where am I? Cambridge, Mass.: MIT Press.

139.   Fredkin, E. (1990). Digital mechanics: An informational process based on reversible universal cellular automata. Physica D 45,254.

140.   Putnam, H. 1975. The meaning of "meaning". In Mind, Language, and Reality. Cambridge: Cambridge University Press.

141. Putnam, H. 1981. Reason, Truth, and History. Cambridge: Cambridge University Press.

142.   Searle, J.R. 1984. Can computers think? In Minds, Brains, and Science. Cambridge, Mass.: Harvard University Press.

143.   Thompson, B. 2003. The Nature of Phenomenal Content. Ph.D. dissertation, University of Arizona.

144.   Wolfram, S. 2002. A New Kind of Science. Champaign, IL: Wolfram Media.

145.   Aho, A.V. and Ullman, J.D. (1992). Foundations of Computer Science,

146.   New York: W.H.Freeman.

147. Baez, J.C. (1995). Spin networks in nonperturbative quantum gravity.

148.   arXiv:gr-qc/9504036 v1 21 Apr 1995. Published in Louis Kauffman (ed.),

149.   The Interface of Knots and Physics, (1996). Providence: A.M.S., pp167-203.

150.   Barrow, J.D., Tipler, F.J. (1986). The Anthropic Cosmological Principle,

151. Oxford and NY: Oxford University Press.

152.   Barrow, J.D. (1991). Theories of Everything. Oxford and NY: Oxford Uni-

153.   versity Press.

154.   Barrow, J.D. (1992). Pi in the Sky, Oxford: Clarendon Press.

155.   Beem, J.K. and Ehrlich, P.E. (1981). Global Lorentzian Geometry, New

156.   York: Dekker.

157. Bekenstein, J.D. (2003). Information in the holographic universe, Scientific

158.   American, August, pp48-55.

159. Bekenstein, J.D. (2004). How does the entropy/information bound work?
160. arXiv:quant-ph/0404042 v1 7 Apr 2004. Besse, A.L. (1987). Einstein manifolds, Berlin and New York: Springer-Verlag.
161. Boothby, W.M. (1986). An introduction to differentiable manifolds and Rie-
162. mannian geometry, 2nd Edition, London: Academic Press.
163. Cornish, N.J., Spergel, D.N., Starkman, G.D. (1998). Circles in the sky:
164. Finding Topology with the Microwave Background Radiation, Classical and
165. Quantum Gravity, Vol.15, No.9, September, pp2657-2670.
166. Dancy, J. (1985). Introduction to Contemporary Epistemology, Oxford: Blackwell. Dancy, J., Sosa, E. (eds.) (1992). A Companion to Epistemology, Oxford: Blackwell.